Portrait Miniatures in National Trust Houses
Volume 2: Cornwall, Devon and Somerset

Portrait Miniatures in National Trust Houses

Volume 2: Cornwall, Devon and Somerset

Richard Walker and Alastair Laing

THE NATIONAL TRUST

First published in Great Britain in 2005.

National Trust Enterprises Ltd
36 Queen Anne's Gate
London SW1H 9AS

www.nationaltrust.org.uk

ISBN 0-7078-0364-0

Cataloguing in Publication Data is available from the British Library.

Designed by Fetherstonhaugh Associates.
www.fetherstonhaugh.com

Printed in the UK by Selwood Printing Ltd., West Sussex

CONTENTS

ACKNOWLEDGEMENTS

The National Trust gratefully acknowledges the financial support of the following organisations, without which publication of this volume would not have been possible:

Furthermore, a programme of the J. M. Kaplan Fund
The Leche Trust
The Marc Fitch Fund
The Paul Mellon Centre for Studies in British Art

The authors could never have accomplished this task without the co-operation and help of a great number of people. But the catalogue itself would be of much less interest had not Sir Richard Carew Pole and his fellow-trustee of the Carew Pole Silver Settlement, and Lord St Levan and James St. Aubyn agreed to the inclusion of the miniatures held in private ownership at Antony and St. Michael's Mount. We owe it to them to say that inclusion in this catalogue does not necessarily imply that all their miniatures are available to public view. However, their inclusion here is vital to understanding the context of those that are. We likewise owe Iona, Lady Molesworth-St. Aubyn and her Administrator, James Reynolds, a debt of gratitude for allowing one of us to inspect miniatures and paintings at Pencarrow in Cornwall that have helped to resolve the identities of some of the miniatures on St. Michael's Mount; and, at the Mount, Mr & Mrs James St. Aubyn for their hospitality, and for having had the case of miniatures taken off the wall and opened up for inspection. We are additionally very grateful to Sir Richard for agreeing to write the foreword to this volume: truly *pollet virtus*.

They have also had helpful advice, and answers to queries, from Gill Brewer at the National Army Museum, Dr Paul Caffrey at the National College of Art & Design in Dublin, Katherine Coombs at the Victoria & Albert Museum, Melva Croal at Manchester City Art Gallery, Captain David Horn at the Guards Museum, Dr Stephen Lloyd at the Scottish National Portrait Gallery, and Sir Oliver Millar. Any errors in the interpretation of these answers are, however, entirely the authors' responsibility. They have further had much assistance from Dr Jane Cunningham and Melanie Blake of the Courtauld Institute's Photographic Survey (with the Witt Library an invaluable resource), and from the staffs and holdings of the National Portrait Gallery Archive and the London Library.

Colleagues of Alastair Laing at the National Trust deserve great thanks for the time and trouble that they have devoted to seeking out often hidden caches of miniatures and making them available for inspection, and to ferreting for information about them. In particular, the two Curators for Devon and Cornwall, Hugh Meller and Jeremy Pearson; but also Katherine Sharp, the former Assistant Historic Buildings Representative for Devon, for special help with the miniatures recently acquired from Sprydon for Killerton. Anthea Morley-Smith cheerfully seconded Hugh Meller in Devon, just as Ginnie Clotworthy was always ready to help in Cornwall. Further thanks are owed to the following staff in the houses covered by this catalogue: John Rolfe (A la Ronde), Philip Brunsdon (Antony), Shelagh Metcalfe (Arlington Court), Mark Agnew and Michael Thomson (Castle Drogo), Shelley Tobin, Charlotte Eddington and Christina Le Fley (Killerton), Andrea Marchington (Lanhydrock), Simon Larkins (Lytes Cary), Vicki Pepper (Overbeck's), Linda Finnemore (Trerice), John McVerry and James Needham (Tyntesfield). Alastair Laing has further been seconded at Queen Anne's Gate by ready and willing assistance from Emile de Bruijn, Amanda Bradley, Francesca Scoones, Helen Wyld, Eileen Kittier and Douglas Brine. Both authors owe an enormous amount to the encouragement and forebearance of their editor, James Parry, and to the amount of devilling done on their behalf by Samantha Wyndham.

They cannot help but end upon a small note of regret. Visitors to the houses of the National Trust in Cornwall, Devon and Somerset will not fail to notice the absence of the much-loved Montacute and Saltram from this book. That is because neither has any miniatures to show. Those at Montacute were presumably withdrawn when the family moved out in 1911, and nothing seems to be known of what they were, or of their subsequent fate. Those at Saltram, which were hung on the wall in frames, were sadly not included in the acquisition of the principal contents of the house in 1957, and remain in the possession of the family. This represents a diminution in the full panoply of the house's collections, but it also illustrates one of the forgotten virtues of miniatures when seen in public collections – that they are portable, and that they were originally for private delectation, rather than for display. A catalogue such as the present one may perhaps compensate a little for the remoteness.

FOREWORD

'Our family transplants itselfe, To grow in other shires' wrote my ancestor Richard Carew in 1602, and it gives me great pleasure to introduce this new volume of portrait miniatures in Cornwall, Devon and Somerset, which shows the interconnections not just of my family, but of many others, in the south west.

There are about twenty-five houses now owned by the National Trust in this area, and you will find 174 portraits here, some never catalogued before. Ranging in date from the sixteenth to the twentieth centuries, they are intimate snapshots of our forebears: some are glamorous, while others show 'warts and all'. Perhaps, unlike the grander portraits that grace many of the National Trust's houses, they are often spontaneous and capture the personality and appearance of the sitter in a direct and intimate way, as he or she were known by their family and close friends. Some were probably painted to commemorate important family occasions; others to remind the recipient of somebody who was away for a long time, perhaps at war. Many were painted to mark a moment in history or to celebrate a family connection. Sometimes they were placed in lockets or other items of personal adornment, while larger ones were framed to become cabinet pictures. Unlike museums, the houses of the National Trust still display the latter in their original context, as groups around fireplaces or in small vitrines or display cases. At Antony we still have the large easel frames, in which about six or eight miniatures are gathered together, and which still have their glazed cotton light-preventing covers.

From St Michael's Mount in Cornwall to Tyntesfield in North Somerset, the range of portraits is extraordinary. At the former is the rare portrait of Charles I with his white beard, probably painted at the time of his trial in 1648 (SMM 4), and at the latter a series of exquisite portraits of the prosperous Gibbs family painted by Queen Victoria's miniature painter, Sir William Ross, between 1849 and 1852 (TYN 18-19 & 23). In between, we find the great gardener, Sir John Heathcoat Amory of Knightshayes Court in Devon, depicted as a young boy in 1898 (KNI 2).

Some of the artists featured in this volume have local connections. Henry Bone (1755-1834), who was born at Truro in Cornwall, became a porcelain painter at the short-lived Cookworthy factory in Plymouth, before moving to London where he was appointed Enamel Painter to George III, George IV and William IV. Similarly, Richard Crosse (1742-1810), who was born at Knowle, near Cullompton in Devon, became well known. Like many West Country men before and since, he left for London, where he studied at William Shipley's drawing school at the Society of Arts. Here, he must have been a contemporary of the more famous miniaturist, Richard Cosway (1742-1821), a fellow Devonian, whose work is not represented here.

The excellent guidebooks produced by the National Trust are of necessity fairly brief and seldom describe miniatures in any detail. Richard Walker and Alastair Laing's catalogue remedies this deficiency and will become essential reading for all those interested in our rich heritage of houses and families, and their cobweb of connections.

Sir Richard Carew Pole, Bt., OBE, DL

A LA RONDE

DEVON

A la Ronde is one of the quirkiest properties belonging to the National Trust. Not only in external appearance – sixteen-sided, with lozenge-shaped windows at every other angle, and topped by an octagonal lantern crowned by an oriental-looking bell-tower – and in its interiors and collections, but also through its creation and transmission, always by and to women, save in the single case of the Rev. Oswald Reichel (ALA 11), who imposed male notions of rationality and modernisation on it, both without and within.

Its creators were Jane Parminter (1750–1811), daughter of the Barnstaple-born, Lisbon-based wine-merchant turned cement-manufacturer, John Parminter (ALA 6), and her first cousin once removed, Mary Parminter (ALA 10). It was the latter who stipulated in her will that only unmarried kinswomen should inherit the property. She left it to two cousins, Sophia (1786–1879) and Jane (1793–1870) Hurlock, who in turn bequeathed it to their niece, Stella Reichel (1837–1923). It was she who, having forfeited her own eligibility by marrying the Rev. John Tudor, broke the trust to transfer A la Ronde to her brother Oswald. After his death in 1923, Stella's daughter Margaret bought it and re-established the principle of female succession, which continued until Ursula Tudor-Perkins sold it to the National Trust in 1991.

It is partly because of this history of succession by women that the collection of miniatures at A la Ronde is a rather haphazard one, but for the core group dating back to the Parminters. This includes a good unfinished late seventeenth-century portrait of Richard (I) Parminter (ALA 2); a fine plumbago drawing probably by the Scottish artist, James Ferguson, of John Parminter (ALA 6); and the best miniature in the house, possibly by Ozias Humphry, of Mary Parminter around 1784 (ALA 10). The miniature is of exceptional quality and shows Mary as a girl, presumably painted for her relatives in England before she embarked with her cousin Jane on the grand tour that lasted from 1784 to 1795, from which they returned to build A la Ronde.

Left: the south side of the house
Right: miniatures in the Dining Room

ALA 1

Lady in a Blue Dress

British School, *c.*1650

HS to left in a blue dress, white chemise with a small blue bow, and a triple pearl necklace. Dark brown eyes, long dark hair in ringlets, very pale (faded) complexion, aged about 30. Plain dark background, lit from the right.

Oil on copper: oval, 54 x 41mm ($2^1/_8$ x $1^5/_8$in). Glazed but unframed.

Prov: uncertain.

The identity of the sitter is unknown. She appears to be a young woman in *c.*1650, crudely painted by a distant follower of Alexander Cooper.

ALAR/P/42

ALA 2

Richard (I) Parminter

British School, *c.*1710–20

HS to left, head turned to front, in a brown coat and white twisted cravat. Dark eyes and eyebrows, long full-bottomed wig (uncoloured), pale face modelled with short blue left-handed strokes, aged about 35. Speckled brown background, lit from the left.

Watercolour and plumbago on copper: oval, 44 x 35mm ($1^3/_4$ x $1^3/_8$in). Oval pinchbeck locket with monogram engraved on the back with the initials: *R.G.P.*.

Prov: presumably by inheritance.

Richard (I) Parminter (*c.*1680/5 (?)–1761) is the first member of the family of whom we have any certain knowledge. He was the grandfather of Jane Parminter, and the great-grandfather of Mary Parminter. His birthdate is not known, but it is likely that, as was customary, he was a little older than his wife, Jane Lavington (1685–1761). He became Recorder of Tiverton in 1748. His eldest son, Richard II, was the grandfather of Mary Parminter (ALA 10), and his next son, John (ALA 6), was the father of Jane.

ALAR/P/18c

ALA 3

Councillor Walrond

British School, *c.*1720

HS to right in a red coat, white neckcloth and cravat. Brown eyes, long grey knotted wig with foretop, dark face modelled with greenish-grey wash. Plain dark grey background, lit from the left.

Ivory: oval, 61 x 44mm ($2^1/_2$ x $1^3/_4$in), inscr. on back of ivory in ink: *Councillor Walrond son of the Rev W. Walrond of Exeter*. Oval silver-gilt frame.

Prov: presumably by inheritance.

The sitter is probably Henry Walrond (d.1747), of Bedford House, Exeter. He was one of the Exeter city councillors and the builder, in *c.*1740, of Tidwell House, Sidmouth. His sister, Mary, m. Samuel Parminter (b.1717). A daughter, or niece, Polly Walrond (1747–1772), m. Richard (III) Parminter (1736–1779); they were the parents of Mary Parminter (ALA 10), one of the builders of A la Ronde. The Walrond Papers in the Devon Record Office (West Country Studies Library) contain a family tree, and the wills of Henry Walrond and his brothers Clement (d.1744) and John (d.1769).

ALAR/P/18f

ALA 4

Young Man in a Grey Coat

British School, *c.*1725–35

HS to right in a grey coat, gold-embroidered waistcoat, white neckcloth and shirt-frill. Brown eyes, grey knotted wig, pale face modelled with coarse blue stipple, aged in his twenties. Plain grey wash background, lit from the left.

Ivory: oval, 45 x 36mm ($1^3/_4$ x $1^1/_2$in), sight size. Oval gilt locket with filigree cresting, and shell motif below.

Prov: uncertain.

The identity of the sitter is uncertain. He appears to be a young man in the 1720s, possibly one of the thirteen children, or a son-in-law, of Richard (I) Parminter (ALA 2) of Bideford (d.1761) and Jane Lavington (1685–1761). The artist was a competent miniaturist, of the school of Christian Richter.

ALAR/P/18d

ALA 5

Man in a Blue Coat

British School, *c.*1740

HS to right in a blue coat with powder on shoulders, brown waistcoat, white neckcloth and shirt-frill. Brown eyes, grey bob wig, fresh face modelled with brown stipple, aged about 50. Plain brown background, lit from the left.

Ivory: oval, 44 x 35mm ($1^3/_4$ x $1^3/_8$in). Oval gilt locket.

Prov: uncertain.

The sitter appears to be a middle-aged man in the 1740s, possibly one of the brothers of Henry Walrond (ALA 3).

ALAR/P/18b

ALA 6

John Parminter

Attributed to James Ferguson, *c.*1740

HS to right in a turban, loose coat, unbuttoned waistcoat, and open shirt-collar, aged about 30.

Plumbago on card (or vellum): oval, 65 x 54mm ($2\frac{5}{8}$ x $2\frac{1}{8}$in), contemporary inscription on backing paper in ink: *Mr John Parminter Senior of Fairlinch*. Oval pear-wood frame.

Prov: presumably by inheritance.

Very similar, and of identical date, to the pen-and-ink drawing by Ferguson of an unknown man, in the V&A Museum, there dated to 1750–60 but possibly earlier. This drawing of John Parminter appears to be of the 1740s.

John (b.1712), second s. of Richard (I) Parminter (d.1761; ALA 2) and Jane Lavington (1685–1761). He m. in *c.*1745, Jane Arbouin or Arboyne (b.1712), and owned a wine export business in Lisbon, where their daughter Jane was born in 1750. The great Lisbon earthquake of 1755 ruined his business, but he managed to market a form of quick-drying cement which was used to rebuild the city, and restored the family fortunes. An oil portrait of him is also at A la Ronde (Octagon).

ALAR/P/8

ALA 7

Rebecca Parminter

British School, *c.*1750

See also colour plate 1.

HS to right, head turned to left, in a blue dress with a blue and white collar, and a white cap with blue bow. Large brown eyes, long brown hair in ringlets on shoulders, pale face modelled with blue stipple, smiling expression, long neck, aged about 15. Plain light grey background.

Ivory: oval, 44 x 30mm ($1\frac{5}{8}$ x $1\frac{1}{8}$in). Oval gold locket with inset dark blue glass or enamel rim and outer bead moulding (formerly a bracelet).

Prov: presumably by inheritance.

A reasonable-quality miniature, in the style of Penelope Carwardine, *c.*1750.

Rebecca (d.*c.*1750), probably the daughter of Richard (II) Parminter (1710–1772) and Rebecca Vowler. She is believed to have died aged 15. There must, however, be residual doubts, about either this belief, or the identity of the sitter. For one would not expect a miniature of a just-dead child to be set in such a colourful way, or to have been mounted in a bracelet.

ALAR/P/18g

ALA 8

Young Man in a Red Coat

Manner of Gervase Spencer, *c.*1760

See also colour plate 1.

HS to right in a red coat, white bow-tie and white lace shirt-front. Brown eyes, grey bag wig, pale face neatly modelled with short blue strokes giving a noticeably blue look to the whole face, aged in his twenties. Plain drab background, lit from the left.

Ivory: oval, 35 x 28mm ($1\frac{1}{2}$ x $1\frac{1}{8}$in), sight size. Oval gold locket with blue enamel inset rim and outer bead moulding.

Prov: uncertain.

The sitter appears to be a young man in the 1760s, so that he could conceivably be Mary Parminter's father, Richard (III) Parminter (1736–1779). The miniature is of high quality, but the artist is also unknown; he could perhaps have been Henry Spicer, a pupil of Gervase Spencer.

ALAR/P/18a

ALA 9

Mrs Life (Mrs Lise?)

British School, 1773

HL to left in a blue dress with bow, and white cap with ruched blue ribbon. Brown eyes, smooth grey hair brushed up, aged about 50. Plain blue-grey background.

Oil on card (ace of clubs): oval, 80 x 65mm ($3\frac{1}{4}$ x $2\frac{5}{8}$in), dated on backboard *1773*, and inscr. on backing paper in ink: *Jan 1773 Mrs Life aunt to my Cousin Jane Parminter of A la Ronde*.

Prov: presumably by inheritance.

The miniature is a crude but firm oil painting of 1773, so is not, strictly speaking, a miniature, but its character, size, and framing entitle it to inclusion here.

The Rev. Oswald Reichel suggested, in 1901, that 'probably this is an Arbouin [Jane Arbouin or Arboyne (b.1712) was the mother of Jane Parminter] not a Parminter, (1) because the Parminter aunts to Jane Parminter would have been older in 1773, and (2) because Mary Parminter, in whose writing the inscription is, would otherwise have described her as her own widow [sic]. O.J. Reichel 2 Feb 1901' (red-ink inscription on back of frame).

ALAR/P/6

ALA 10

Mary Parminter

Attributed to Ozias Humphry, *c.*1784

HS to right in a pale blue dress and white diaphanous shawl fastened with a brooch. Hazel eyes, dark brown hair, ruddy complexion, aged about 18. Greenish-drab gouache background, lit from the left.

Ivory: oval, 58 x 46mm ($2\frac{1}{4}$ x $1\frac{7}{8}$in). Oval gold locket with dark hair in the back surrounding a white enamel oval with true-love knot, laurel wreath and a blue enamel circle with initial *P* in seed pearls.

Prov: presumably by inheritance.

The miniature is of very good quality and can be dated to *c.*1784. Ozias Humphry's name is put forward here as a possibility, but without much conviction. He was a Devonian (born in Honiton), but by this time he had long been working in London, and in oils.

Mary (1767–1849), d. of Richard (III) Parminter (1736–1779) and Polly Walrond (1747–1772). She accompanied her cousins, Jane and Elizabeth Parminter, on their tour abroad in 1784, and after their return in 1795, Jane and Mary combined to build A la Ronde. Foreign travel was evidently in their gene pool: Daniel and Samuel Lysons, writing in *Magna Britannia: Devon* (1820), pp. clxxix-clxxx, say of Jane and Elizabeth's brother: 'Mr John Parminter, who, if living, is the representative of the family, is supposed to be leading a wandering life on the

continent.' [We are grateful to Hugh Meller for this reference]. Mary Parminter died unmarried in 1849, leaving a complicated will, stipulating, amongst other things, that A la Ronde should pass only to unmarried female relations, and leaving it to two of them, Jane and Sophia Hurlock. A silhouette of Mary Parminter is also at A la Ronde (Music Room lobby).

ALAR/P/18e

ALA 11

The Rev. Oswald Reichel as a small child

British School, 1842

TQL as a child in a white dress and large blue hat, holding an ivory ring on a blue ribbon.

Oil on mahogany: rectangle, 74 x 62mm (2⁷/₈ x 2¹/₂in), inscr: *aetat 2 A.D. 1842*. Circular wood easel-frame, chipped at bottom.

Prov: probably commissioned by his parents in 1842, from a local artist, and then by inheritance.

Oswald J. Reichel (1840–1923), eldest s. of the Rev. Samuel Reichel (1787–1857) of Ockbrook, Derbyshire, by his second wife, Matilda (1798–1871), d. of Joseph Hurlock (1754–1845) of Oxted, Surrey. Ordained in 1865, when he became curate of North Hinksey and Vice-Principal of Cuddesdon College, Oxford, until 1869/70, when he became Vicar of Sparsholt with Kingston Lisle, Berkshire. In 1886 he retired to A la Ronde, which he obtained from his sister, Stella, lived there for thirty-seven years, and made many substantial alterations, including replacing the thatch with tiles, adding dormer windows, and installing a gargantuan central heating system. He devoted his retirement to antiquarian and ecclesiastical study, contributing no less than thirty-seven papers to the *Transactions* of the Devonshire Association, and publishing *A Complete Manual of Canon Law* (1896–1900).

ALAR/D/10

ANTONY

CORNWALL

Antony contains one of the most interesting collections of miniatures in the care of the National Trust. They are mainly of members of the Carew and Pole-Carew families (there is only one pure Pole), and range in date from close to the start of the art of miniature painting in the sixteenth century, right up to Victorian times. Unfortunately, because of the very remote relationship through which the Carew seat, Antony, was inherited by Reginald Pole of Stoke Damerel, Devon, (who thereupon took the name of Pole-Carew), following the demise of the Carews in the male line with the death of John Carew of Crowcombe in 1771, the identities of the sitters in many of the earlier miniatures became muddled, or were lost altogether. The earliest, ANT 1, is a splendid portrait by Nicholas Hilliard, dated 1587, of Charles Blount, 1st Earl of Devonshire, one of Queen Elizabeth's favourites and an intrepid soldier. Hilliard's son, Laurence, painted a fine portrait of Lord Keeper Coventry around 1625 (ANT 2), and a cheerful young widow about ten years later (ANT 4). The miniature by John Hoskins the Younger of a Commonwealth woman, defying the puritan approval of restraint in clothes and jewellery, is an illuminating specimen of this mysterious artist's work (ANT 6). But the pride of the Antony collection is surely the two Samuel Cooper miniatures thought to be of John Carew the regicide and of Sarah Hungerford, the first wife of Sir John Carew, 3rd Bt. These marvellously perceptive portraits, by one of the greatest English artists, were painted just before and after the Restoration (ANT 9 & 10). A good example of the work of John Smart, the great eighteenth-century miniaturist, is his portrait of Admiral Sir Charles Pole as a young post-captain in 1785 (ANT 23), and a particularly attractive nineteenth-century miniature, by Annie Dixon, is of the Pole-Carew children, Geraldine, Reginald and Julia, admiring a bird's nest (ANT 34). None of these miniatures belongs to the National Trust, and not all of them are on public view.

Left: the south front
Right: the Library

ANT 1

Charles Blount, 8th (and last) Lord Mountjoy, Earl of Devonshire, K.G.

Nicholas Hilliard, 1587

HS to left in a buff doublet, lace collar over a steel cuirass, gold chain, and a jewelled ear-ring. Pale grey eyes, curly brown hair, small moustache, very pale face, aged 24. Dark blue background inscr. in gold: *Amor amoris premium .. / Año Dmni 1587.*

Vellum: oval, 43 x 35mm ($1\frac{3}{4}$ x $1\frac{3}{8}$in). Gold locket, 51 x 38mm (2 x $1\frac{1}{2}$in) with spiral crest and blank scroll.

Prov: uncertain.

Exh: SKM 1865 (359); V&A Museum 1947 (34); Manchester 1953 (34); RA 1956–7 (622); The Hague 1958 (8); NMM 1988 (13.29).

Lit: Auerbach 1961; Reynolds 1971; Edmond 1983.

This may be counted among the great Elizabethan portraits. Auerbach (1961, p.199) describes it as one of Hilliard's finest works, with excellent lettering and an exquisite rendering of armour and lace collar.

Charles Blount (1563–1606), created Earl of Devonshire (or Devon) by James I in 1603. He was one of Queen Elizabeth's favourites and served with distinction in the Netherlands, the Armada campaign, in Brittany and in Ireland. As a young man, that is, at the time of this miniature, he was 'of a brown hair, a sweet face, a most neat composure and tall in his person'. One of his illegitimate sons by Lady Penelope Rich, Mountjoy, was created Earl of Newport, and played an important, if ambiguous, role in the Civil War; he was painted in various ways by Van Dyck, twice with Lord Goring (the original of one version is at Petworth House [NT], and a copy of the other is at Knole [NT]).

CI.61b

ANT 2

Lord Keeper Coventry

Attributed to Laurence Hilliard, c.1625

See also colour plate 1.

HS to right in a black robe and large white ruff, holding Seal bag. Pale brown eyes, short black hair, trim beard and moustache, pale face, aged about 45 to 50. Plain blue background, lit from the left.

Card: oval, 52 x 42mm (2 x $1\frac{5}{8}$in), inscr. in gold letters: *Dominus Thomas Coventrie, Custos-Sigilli / Ditissimus Thesaurus Cordis Conscientia Sana.* Crested gold locket with scroll engr.: *LORD KEEPER COVENTRY*, and a paper label on the back inscr. in ink: *Isaac Oliver* erased, and *L. Hilliard* substituted in pencil.

Prov: presumably by descent.

Exh: SKM 1865 (360).

In the 1865 exhibition at South Kensington this was attributed to Nicholas Hilliard, and later to Isaac Oliver, but the more recent attribution to Laurence Hilliard is the most likely. It was possibly painted in 1625, when Thomas Coventry was appointed Lord Keeper.

Thomas Coventry (1578–1640), son of Sir Thomas Coventry, Justice of Common Pleas. He was appointed Attorney-General in 1621 and Lord Keeper in 1625, and created 1st Baron Coventry in 1628. His moderating influence on Charles I was cut short by his untimely death in 1640. A portrait of him in oils, after the Cornelius Jonson at Longleat House, Wiltshire, is also at Antony. The daughter and heiress of his great-grandson, Gilbert, 4th Earl of Coventry, m. Sir William Carew, 5th Baronet, in 1713.

CI.62d

ANT 3

Frederick Henry, Prince of Orange

Dutch School, after Michel Van Miereveldt, c.1625

HS to right in a red and gold doublet, and falling lace collar. Dark eyes, long dark brown hair, light brown beard and moustache, aged about 40. Plain dark background, lit from the left.

Oil on copper: oval, 48 x 39mm ($1\frac{7}{8}$ x $1\frac{1}{2}$in), sight size. Plain gold locket with scroll engr.: *FRED: PRINCE OF ORANGE.*

Prov: uncertain.

Cornelius Jonson has been suggested as the artist, but the portrait is very close to a miniature by Henri Toutin in the Mauritshuis, The Hague, and both are probably adapted from the full-sized oil by Miereveldt in the Rijksmuseum, Amsterdam.

Frederick Henry (1583/4–1647), youngest son of William the Silent. He m. in 1625, Amalia, Countess of Solms, and later in the same year succeeded his elder brother Maurice as Stadholder of the United Provinces.

CI.63c

ANT 4
Lady in a Black Dress
Laurence Hilliard, *c.*1635–40

HS to right in a low-cut black dress, widow's peak, pearl necklace and ear-rings. Brown eyes, dark brown hair in ringlets and forehead curls, rosy complexion, smiling expression, aged about 40. Gouache green and blue grass and sky background, lit from the left.

Card: oval, 70 x 52mm ($2\frac{3}{4}$ x 2in), signed lower right in gold paint with initials: *L.H.* Plain gilt locket with blank scroll.

Prov: uncertain.

Exh: SKM 1865 (401).

A fine example of an initialled miniature by Nicholas Hilliard's son, Laurence, who signed his work infrequently. The sitter appears to be a young and cheerful widow of the late 1630s, although it is possible that the transparent widow's peak may be a later addition. The square-cut décolleté dress and distinctive hair-style with profuse ringlets may be seen in Van Dyck's portrait of Queen Henrietta Maria in the Royal Collection (Millar 1963, No.148).

CI.62b

ANT 5
Portrait of a Young Lady
Manner of John Hoskins, *c.*1650

HL to right holding roses, in a black dress, broad white pointed collar, and white cuffs, with a gold ring on third finger of her right hand. Light brown eyes, gold hair tied with black ribbon, aged about 20 to 25. Plain grey background.

Vellum: oval, 55 x 45mm ($2\frac{1}{8}$ x $1\frac{3}{4}$in), sight size. Oval black wood frame with typed label behind: *BY JOHN HOSKINS CIRCA 1620.*

Prov: uncertain.

The sitter appears to be a young woman in the 1650s, possibly English. The plain linen collar, or kerchief, draped over the shoulders is in marked contrast to the sumptuous ruffs of fashionable circles and suggests that the subject might be a merchant's wife or daughter of that period. The name of John Hoskins attached to the miniature is possible, if optimistic, but there is something slightly Dutch about it.

ANT/M/1/1

ANT 6
Lady in a Blue Dress
John Hoskins the Younger, *c.*1650–55

HL facing in a blue dress, yellow and grey patterned cloak, pearl necklace and large ear-drops. Grey eyes, long fair hair in ringlets and dressed with jewels, pale complexion. Background dark to left, pale blue to right, lit from the left.

Card: oval, 62 x 49mm ($2\frac{1}{2}$ x $1\frac{7}{8}$in), signed mid-left with initials: *I.H.* on a dark ground. Crested gold locket with blank scroll.

Prov: uncertain.

The identity of the sitter is unknown, but the portrait is a good example of John Hoskins the Younger's work in the 1650s, escaping from the formality of the Hilliard tradition. She appears to be a young woman in *c.*1650–55 (*cf.* NPG 1974 (23) and Murdoch et al. 1981, Fig.120), or possibly even later. A comparable miniature, dated 1660, is at Ickworth in Suffolk (NT).

CI.61d

ANT 7
Man in a Black Coat
Style of Samuel Cooper, *c.*1650–60

HS to right in a black coat and white shallow curved collar. Brown eyes, long dark hair, pale face, aged about 30. Plain greenish drab background, lit from the left.

Green playing-card: oval, 59 x 49mm ($2\frac{3}{8}$ x $1\frac{7}{8}$in). Plain gilt locket with blank scroll.

Prov: uncertain.

Exh: probably SKM 1865 (357) as 'Portrait of a Gentleman. Time of Charles II'.

The miniature is of good quality, by a close follower of Samuel Cooper, possibly Richard Gibson. The identity of the sitter is unknown. He appears to be a young man in the 1650s, wearing an interesting curved collar without tassels or strings.

CI.62a

ANT 8
Young Man in Armour
British School, *c.*1660–70

HS slightly to right, in armour and white lace cravat.

Card: oval, 42 x 34mm ($1\frac{5}{8}$ x $1\frac{3}{8}$in). Oval gold locket with spiral crest and blank scroll.

Prov: uncertain.

Exh: possibly SKM 1865 (357) as 'Portrait of a Gentleman. Time of Charles II. Card'.

The identity of the sitter is unknown. He appears to be a young officer in the 1660s, painted by an artist in the circles of Nicholas Dixon and Peter Cross.

CI.61a

ANT 9

Called 'Sir John Carew'

Samuel Cooper, *c.*1660

See also colour plate 2.

HS to left in armour and white scarf. Dark brown eyes, long bushy brown hair, slight moustache, aged about 30 to 35. Dark blue background.

Vellum: oval, 74 x 62mm ($2\frac{7}{8}$ x $2\frac{1}{2}$in). Crested gold locket with scroll engr.: *SIR JOHN CAREW.*

Prov: uncertain.

Exh: SKM 1865 (361); RA 1960–61 (591, as of 'Sir' John Carew, d.1660); NPG 1974 (73, as ditto).

Lit: Foskett 1974 (No.30, as of 'Sir' John Carew, d.1660).

A magnificent example of Samuel Cooper's work of *c.*1660, despite its by then archaic use of a plain azure background (but *cf.* the signed miniature thought to be of *Lady Denham* in the Buccleuch Collection: Foskett 1974, col.pl.7). The over-the-shoulder pose is also a most unusual one for Cooper to have employed for a male sitter (but *cf.* the signed and dated miniature of *Hugh May* of 1653 in the Royal Collection, and the signed and dated one of *George Vernon* of 1660, in family possession).

These comparisons, together with the hairstyle and knotted white stock over armour, suggest the date of around 1660, but it is here that difficulties over the sitter's true identity arise. The gilt scroll calls him 'Sir John Carew', which could only signify the 3rd Baronet (1635–92). Not only does the sitter seem a little old for him, even in the early 1660s, but there is also no resemblance to the better-attested likeness of the 3rd Bt. in the portrait in oils by Riley, also at Antony. There is also no rapport with the Cooper miniature supposedly of his first wife (ANT 10).

Since the *Age of Charles II* exhibition in 1960–61, there has been a tendency to identify 'Sir John Carew' with his half-uncle, John the regicide (b.*c.*1622; executed 1660), ignoring the fact that he was never knighted. Even so, this might have been more plausible, but for the fact that he was a Fifth Monarchist, and that he lived in seclusion upon his estates between his imprisonment in St. Mawes Castle in 1655, and his proceeding to London for trial in 1660. The doubts are a pity, since one would so much like this to be the image of the 'republican without guile and reproach' (*DNB*).

Cl.61e

ANT 10

? Sarah (Hungerford), Lady Carew

Samuel Cooper, *c.*1662

See also colour plate 2.

HS to right in a low-cut crimson dress, grey cloak, and large pearl necklace. Brown eyes, long brownish hair smooth on top, very pale face, aged about 25. Sky and landscape background, darker to left.

Vellum: oval, 59 x 47mm ($2\frac{3}{8}$ x $1\frac{7}{8}$in), signed mid-left with monogram: *SC* on dark ground. Crested gold locket with scroll engr.: *LADY CAREW.*

Prov: uncertain.

Exh: SKM 1865 (364); RA 1960–61 (589, as 'Lady Carew', wife of the regicide); NPG 1974 (74, as ditto).

Lit: Foskett 1974, p.121 (as 'Lady Carew').

The two miniatures, ANT 9 and ANT 10, do not constitute a pair, and there is similar doubt about the identity of the woman (a second signed version in the V&A Museum is reproduced in colour in Murdoch 1997, p.145, pl.9B, as of '*A Lady Carew*', although it was given to the Museum by Alexander Dyer in 1869 as a portrait of '*Cooper's wife*'). Nevertheless, this miniature is among Samuel Cooper's most accomplished works, painted shortly after the Restoration.

Sarah (d.1671), daughter of Antony Hungerford of Farleigh Castle, Somerset. She m. before 1664, as his first wife, Sir John Carew, 3rd Bt., (1635–92), and bore him two daughters: Jane (d.1700), who married Jonathan Rashleigh of Menabilly, and whose daughter Sarah, by her marriage to the Rev. Charles Pole, became the progenitor of the Pole-Carews; and Rachel, who died unmarried in 1705, and became the heroine of Daphne du Maurier's *My Cousin Rachel.*

Cl.61f

ANT 11

Portrait of a Man

British School, *c.*1680–90

HS slightly to left in a voluminous white cravat. Dark eyes, long brown hair, double chin, frowning expression, aged about 60. Dark background.

Oil on card: oval, 50 x 40mm (2 x $1\frac{5}{8}$in), sight size. Crested gold locket with blank scroll.

Prov: uncertain.

Exh: possibly SKM 1865 (356) as 'Portrait of a Gentleman. Time of Charles II. Oil'.

The identity of the sitter is unknown. He appears to be a middle-aged, well-dressed man in the 1680s, possibly Dutch. Sir Oliver Millar suggests it may be after a portrait by Pieter Borssalaer, who worked as a portrait painter in England in the 1670s, known as Peter Bustler. There are, indeed, affinities with the head of the TQL in oils by Borssalaer of *Admiral Cornelius Tromp* (1675) at Antony.

Cl.61c

ANT 12

Young Man in Armour

British School, *c.*1685

HS to right in armour and a broad lace cravat over a large black bow. Brown eyes, dark brown hair, pale puffy face, aged about 25. Plain grey background, lit from the left.

Card: oval, 67 x 54mm ($2\frac{5}{8}$ x $2\frac{1}{8}$in), sight size. Crested gold locket with blank scroll, and paper label on the back inscr.: *Unknown Circa Charles I* [sic].

Prov: uncertain.

Exh: SKM 1865 (398) as 'time of Charles I'.

The identity of the sitter is unknown, but the distinctive combination of cravat and flat black bow was popular for men in the 1680s. Could he be Jonathan Rashleigh (d.1702) of Menabilly, who m. Jane Carew in 1681? One might expect a likeness of him here, since their daughter, Sarah, married the Rev. Charles Pole in 1714, and was the grandmother of Reginald Pole (1753–1835), who took the additional name of Carew after inheriting Antony, and from whom the Pole-Carews were descended.

CI.63a

ANT 13

Man in a Red Coat

British School, *c.*1690

HS to left in a red coat and white cravat. Brown eyes, long brown hair, aged about 35. Dark background, lit from the right.

Oil on copper: oval, 58 x 44mm ($2\frac{1}{4}$ x $1\frac{3}{4}$in), with green playing-card backing. Plain gilt locket with blank scroll.

Prov: uncertain.

Exh: possibly SKM 1865 (363) as 'Portrait of a Gentleman, Oil. Copper'.

The identity of the sitter is unknown. He appears to be a well-dressed young man in the 1690s.

CI.62c

ANT 14

Gertrude (Carew), Lady Copley

Style of Christian Richter, *c.*1705

HS slightly to left in a blue low-cut dress and white chemise. Brown eyes, long dark hair, pale face, aged about 25. Plain dark grey background, lit from the left.

Card: oval, 72 x 59mm ($2\frac{7}{8}$ x $2\frac{3}{8}$in). Plain gold locket with scroll engr.: *DAUGHTER OF SIR JOHN CAREW.*

Prov: presumably by descent.

Exh: SKM 1865 (402), unattributed.

The flat, slightly stiff treatment of the paint suggests the work of Richter rather than Bernard Lens.

Gertrude (1682–1736), youngest daughter of Sir John Carew, 3rd Bt., and his only daughter by his third wife, Mary Morice. She m. firstly, as his second wife, Sir Godfrey Copley, 2nd Bt., around 1700, and secondly, in or before 1718, Sir Coplestone Warwick Bampfylde, 3rd Bt.

This miniature derives from a painted oval in oils by Charles D'Agar, which is also at Antony.

CI.63f

ANT 15

Prince James, 'The Old Pretender'

19th century (?), after an original of *c.*1704–8

HS to left in armour edged with blue, red and gold, the Garter riband, and a white knotted cravat. Dark brown eyes, long powdered wig, aged about 20. Plain dark background, lit from the left.

Ivory: oval, 68 x 51mm ($2\frac{3}{4}$ x 2in), sight size. Plain gold locket with scroll engr.: *THE OLD CHEVALIER.*

Prov: uncertain.

Exh: SKM 1865 (367).

Lit: Kerslake 1977, p.157; Walker 1992, p.72.

This appears to be a late derivative (it is painted on ivory, rather than on card or vellum) of the print by Pierre Simon, which is known in two states, the first of which is undated (for this, *see* exh. cat. *La Cour des Stuarts à Saint-Germain-en-Laye au temps de Louis XIV*, Musée des Antiquités nationales de Saint-Germain-en-Laye, 1992, no.65), and the second, reissued at the time of the planned Franco-Jacobite invasion of Scotland, is dated 1708 (*cf.* Sharp 1996, cat.124 (ii), p.91-92 and fig.). Although Simon's image is sometimes said to be taken from one of the many miniatures of James III by Jacques-Antoine Arlaud, it is actually closer to those by Anne Chéron (*cf.* Corp 2001, pp.45-46, 107, and fig.23). These date from 1704.

James Francis Edward Stuart (1688–1766), only son of James II and Mary of Modena, known to his Jacobite adherents as James III. He employed the incognito of the 'Chevalier de St George' in France.

CI.63e

ANT 16
Letitia Trelawney
Bernard Lens, *c.*1720–30

See also colour plate 1.

HL to left, head tilted to right, in a beige and gold dress, blue cloak, and string of pearls over her left breast. Grey eyes, long dark brown hair, pale face, aged about 25. Plain grey background, lit from the left.

Ivory: oval, 78 x 64mm ($3^1/_8$ x $2^1/_2$in), signed lower left with gold monogram: *BL*. Plain gold locket with scroll engr.: *LATITIA* [sic] *DAUGHTER OF THE / REVD SIR I. TRELAWNEY*.

Prov: see below.

A good example of a Bernard Lens miniature of the 1720s, possibly based on a portrait by Michael Dahl.

Letitia (*c.*1700–75), daughter of the Right Rev. Sir Jonathan Trelawney, 3rd Bt. and Bishop of Exeter. She m. in 1720 her cousin, Sir Henry Trelawney, 5th Bt. Letitia's sister, Rebecca, m. John Buller of Morval. It seems likely that this miniature, like the wax reliefs and plumbago drawings of Bullers in the Library at Antony, came into the family via Anne Buller, wife of Reginald Pole.

CI.63d

ANT 17
Sir Coventry Carew, 6th and last Bt.
Attributed to William Prewett, *c.*1735

HS to right in a crimson coat and waistcoat, and white cravat. Hazel eyes, grey wig, aged about 18 to 20. Plain dark background, lit from the left.

Card: oval, 45 x 36mm ($1^3/_4$ x $1^3/_8$in). Plain gold locket with scroll engr.: *SIR COVENTRY CAREW*.

Prov: uncertain, but probably commissioned by his parents.

Exh: SKM 1865 (394), attributed to Bernard Lens.

In the 1865 SKM exhibition, this miniature and its companion, ANT 18, were both attributed to Bernard Lens, but the style is closer to that of C.F. Zincke, and they are probably by one of Zincke's followers, perhaps Noah Seeman or William Prewett (*cf.* Foskett 1987, p.173, pl.39H).

Coventry (?1716–1748), son of Sir William Carew and Lady Anne Coventry. He succeeded his father as 6th Bt. in 1744, and m. in 1738, as her first husband, his cousin Mary, daughter of Sir Coplestone Warwick Bampfylde, 3rd Bt., of Poltimore, Devon. A portrait of him, attributed to Edward Penny, is also at Antony (*Antony* 1992, p.43). At his death without issue in 1748, Antony passed to Reginald Pole of Stoke Damerel, great-grandson of Sir John Carew, 3rd Bt.

CI.64a

ANT 18
Sir Coventry Carew, 6th Bt. (identity doubtful)
Attributed to William Prewett, *c.*1735

HS facing in a blue coat, white choker and shirt-frill. Hazel eyes, short grey wig, aged about 15. Plain drab background, lit from the left.

Card: oval, 48 x 38mm ($1^7/_8$ x $1^1/_2$in). Plain gold locket with scroll engr.: *SIR COVENTRY CAREW*.

Prov: uncertain, but probably commissioned by his parents.

Exh: SKM 1865 (396).

Since 1865 both this and its companion miniature, ANT 17, have been identified as Sir Coventry Carew, but it seems likely that this one may be of a younger brother who died young, without his existence being recorded in family genealogies.

CI.64b

ANT 19
Mary (Bampfylde), Lady Carew
Attributed to William Prewett, *c.*1738

HS facing in a blue dress edged with white lace. Dark blue eyes, long powdered hair, very pale face, aged about 25. Plain drab background, lit from the left.

Card: oval, 45 x 36mm ($1^3/_4$ x $1^3/_8$in). Plain gold locket with scroll engr.: *LADY CAREW*.

Prov: uncertain.

Exh: SKM 1865 (395).

This and its companion miniatures, ANT 17 and ANT 18, all appear to have been painted by the same hand, but the portrait of Lady Carew may have been done later, in 1738, at the time of her marriage.

Mary (d.1766), daughter of Sir Coplestone Warwick Bampfylde, 3rd Bt., of Poltimore, Devon. She m. in 1738, Sir Coventry Carew, and subsequently, in 1749, Francis Buller of Morval. A portrait of her, by Edward Penny, is also at Antony (*Antony* 1992, p.43).

CI.64

ANT 20
Sir William Carew, 5th Bt.
Circle of Christian Richter, *c.*1735–40

HS to right in a crimson velvet coat, white shirt and white lace cravat. Light brown eyes, long powdered wig, stout face modelled with grey stipple, aged about 50. Plain blue background, lit from the left.

Card: oval, 71 x 55mm ($2^3/_4$ x $2^1/_8$in), possibly signed with initials lower right. Plain gold locket with scroll engr.: *SIR W. CAREW*.

Prov: presumably by descent.

Exh: SKM 1865 (399), unattributed.

This miniature has been ascribed to Benjamin Arlaud, but the attribution is difficult to sustain. The sitter appears to be a man of about 50 in the 1730s, and if the identification with Sir William Carew is correct, probably nearer 1740. Benjamin Arlaud is not known to have been active much after 1717, and probably died in 1720. An artist in the circle of Christian Richter is possibly more likely.

William (1689–1744), succeeded his brother, Richard, as 5th Bt. in 1703. He was MP for Saltash and Cornwall 1711–44, and m. in 1713, Lady Anne Coventry, only daughter and heir of Gilbert, 4th Earl of Coventry. A portrait of Sir William, by Michael Dahl, is also at Antony (*Antony* 2002, p.31). Sir William was the builder of the present house at Antony (carcase, 1718–21; finished internally, 1724), the project being greatly assisted by the Coventry inheritance in 1719.

CI.63b

ANT 21

Lady in a Striped Dress

Zeich, after an original of *c.*1780 (?)

HS to left in a low-cut brown dress, with a grey and white striped panel and scarf, and a large mob cap. Grey eyes, long powdered hair, rosy (rouged) complexion, aged about 25. Plain drab background, lit from the left.

Ivory: oval, 48 x 38mm ($1\frac{7}{8}$ x $1\frac{1}{2}$in), said to be signed: *Zeich*. Plain gold locket with blank scroll.

Prov: uncertain.

Exh: SKM 1865 (397).

The SKM 1865 exhibition catalogue stated that this miniature is signed 'Zeich', but the signature cannot be detected at present. Zeich was a nineteenth-century Polish miniaturist. The sitter appears to be a young woman (perhaps an actress), depicted *c.*1780. It could be a copy or a pastiche of a late-eighteenth-century miniature. The way in which the dress does not seem to be properly understood suggests the latter.

Cl.64e

ANT 22

Sir Joseph Yorke, Lord Dover, K.B.

Attributed to Philip Jean, or possibly to John Alefounder, *c.*1780–90

HS to left in Guards uniform (red with blue lapels), black neckcloth, white shirt frill, and star of KB. Grey eyes, short grey bag wig, greenish complexion, aged about 60. Scumbled background, darker to right.

Ivory: oval, 60 x 47mm ($2\frac{3}{8}$ x $1\frac{7}{8}$in). Plain gold locket with scroll engr.: *SIR J. YORKE LORD DOVER*.

Prov: doubtless by gift to, and inheritance from, the sitter's niece, Jemima Yorke, first wife of the Right Hon. Reginald Pole-Carew.

Exh: SKM 1865 (393).

The miniature was unattributed in the SKM 1865 exhibition, and the ascription to Alefounder seems to be relatively modern, although little of his work is available from which to form a judgement. The sitter appears to be aged about 60, and the style of his clothes and wig suggest the 1780s, possibly at the time of his marriage in 1783, or when he was raised to the peerage in 1788, or became Colonel of the Life Guards in 1789. Another version, also attributed to Philip Jean, was sold at Christie's, 27 February 1968 (103). Were the miniature to be by Alefounder, it would have to have been done before 1785, when he set off for India, where, after many disappointments, he committed suicide with a pen-knife on Christmas Day, 1794 (*cf.* Archer 1979, pp.270-72).

Joseph Yorke (1724–92), third son of Lord Chancellor Hardwicke. He had a distinguished army career in the 9th Foot Regiment, 8th and 5th Dragoons, 11th Light Dragoons, and finally the 1st Regiment of Life Guards. He was ADC to the Duke of Cumberland at the Battle of Fontenoy (1745). He was also ambassador in The Hague and Paris, KB 1761, and was created Baron Dover in 1788. He m. in 1783, Christina, Baroness de Stöcken, of Denmark. A copy in oils by J.S. Webster of the TQL of Lord Dover by Guillaume Spinny was recently acquired for Wimpole Hall (NT).

Cl.64d

ANT 23

Admiral Sir Charles Morice Pole, Bt.

John Smart, 1785

HS to right in a blue coat with brass buttons, white neckcloth and shirt frill. Hazel eyes, short grey wig in queue, ruddy face, aged 28.

Paper: oval, 60 x 48mm ($2\frac{3}{8}$ x $1\frac{7}{8}$in), signed lower left: *J.S. / 1785*. Plain gold locket with scroll engr.: *ADM. SIR C. POLE*.

Prov: presumably by gift and descent.

Exh: SKM 1865 (392).

Lit: Foskett 1964, p.72.

A characteristically elegant example of Smart's work of the 1780s, before he left for India in April 1785. Charles Pole was a post captain at this time. This must have been one of the miniatures that detained Smart in England, giving Ozias Humphry, who greatly feared the competition from him in India, and who set off in January 1785, a head start (*cf.* Williamson 1918, pp.118-19, 126-27, & 129-30).

Charles Morice (1757–1830), second son of Reginald Pole of Stoke Damerel and Anne Buller. Entered the navy in 1772, commanded ships in Newfoundland and the Baltic, Admiral of the Fleet 1830. Made a baronet in 1801; GCB 1818. He m. Henrietta Goddard, by whom he had two daughters, the elder of whom married Sir William Stuart of Tempsford Hall, Bedfordshire, but no son, so the baronetcy expired with him.

Cl.64f

ANT 24

William Henry, 3rd Lord Lyttelton

Sir William Newton, *c.*1805–10

HL to right in a brown top coat trimmed with brown fur, yellow waistcoat, high white neckcloth and white shirt frill. Brown eyes, short black hair and side-whiskers, creamy skin, aged between 20 and 25. Tempestuous sky background.

Ivory: rectangle with rounded top corners, 108 x 81mm ($4\frac{1}{4}$ x $3\frac{1}{4}$in), sight size. Silver-gilt rectangular frame with convex glass and tablet behind engr.: *Hon. W. Lyttelton afterwards 3rd Baron Lyttelton*, and typescript label: *BY SIR WILLIAM NEWTON*.

Prov: probably by gift to the sitter's brother-in-law, the Rt. Hon. Reginald Pole-Carew, and then by descent.

The miniature dates from *c.*1805–10 and is one of Newton's earliest portraits. It was possibly painted to celebrate the sitter's election as a Member of Parliament in 1806.

William Henry (1782–1837), third son of Sir William Henry Lyttelton, 7th Bt. and 1st Baron Lyttelton and his second wife, Caroline Bristow. He was MP for Worcestershire 1806–20, and succeeded his half-brother as 3rd Baron Lyttelton in 1828. He m. in 1813, Lady Sarah Spencer (*see* ANT 27), daughter of George John, 2nd Earl Spencer. His sister, the Hon. Caroline Lyttelton, m. in 1808, the Rt. Hon. Reginald Pole-Carew of Antony (*see* ANT 25 & 26).

ANT/MI/1/4

ANT 25

The Hon. Caroline Lyttelton, Mrs Reginald Pole-Carew

Elizabeth Paye, 1808

See also colour plate 1.

HS to right in a dark grey dress, square white lace collar, and coral necklace. Hazel eyes, luxuriant curly black hair with crimson band, high complexion, aged 31. Dark brown background, lit from the left.

Ivory: rectangle, 77 x 62mm (3 x 2$^{1}/_{2}$in), sight size. Rectangular gilt-metal frame mounted on black wood with leaf and berry suspension, and typed label behind: *The Hon. Mrs C.A. Pole Carew. Painted by Miss Paye (afterwards Mrs Bryane) 1808.*

Prov: presumably by descent.

This is a skilfully painted and attractive miniature, showing the sitter with a long neck and a slight smile, and is neatly modelled with blue-grey paint and dramatic chiaroscuro. It was painted in 1808, probably as an engagement or wedding present. An enamel copy, by H.P. Bone (1833), is at Hagley Hall (Viscount Cobham).

Caroline Anne (1777–1838), elder child and only daughter of the second marriage of William Henry, 1st Baron Lyttelton. She m. in 1808, as his second wife, the Rt. Hon. Reginald Pole-Carew, who was born Reginald Pole, but added the name of Carew to his own in 1772, after succeeding to Antony in 1769 and following the death of John Carew of Crowcombe in 1771. They had two sons and four daughters. Their elder son, William Henry Pole-Carew (1811–88), succeeded to Antony after Reginald's only surviving son by his first marriage, Joseph Pole-Carew (*see* ANT 28) died in 1852, leaving only a daughter.

ANT/M/1/5

ANT 26

The Hon. Caroline Lyttelton, Mrs Reginald Pole-Carew

Elizabeth Paye, 1808

HS to right in a dark grey dress, square white lace collar, and coral necklace. Hazel eyes, luxuriant curly black hair with crimson band, high complexion, aged 31. Dark brown background, lit from the left.

Ivory: rectangle, 77 x 62mm (3 x 2$^{1}/_{2}$in). Gilt-metal frame with brass label behind engr.: *Hon. Caroline Lyttelton m. Rt Hon. Reginald Pole Carew,* and typed label: *By Miss Paye (afterwards Mrs Bryane) 1808.*

Prov: presumably by descent.

An autograph replica of ANT 25, but a little faded. A third example of this miniature is at Lanhydrock, where it has up until now been wrongly identified as a portrait of the sitter's daughter, Juliana, Lady Robartes (*see* LAN 7).

ANT/M/3/5

ANT 27

Lady Sarah Spencer, later Lady Sarah Lyttelton

Emma Eleonora Kendrick, *c.*1810–15

HL seated to left on a red sofa, in a white flowery dress edged with blue, and four-string necklace, left hand to throat. Brown eyes, dark hair in ringlets, pinned up at back with red ribbon, aged about 25.

Ivory: rectangle, 71 x 55mm (2$^{3}/_{4}$ x 2$^{1}/_{8}$in). Rectangular silver-gilt frame engr. behind: *Lady Sarah Spencer afterwards Lady Lyttelton,* and typed label: *by Emma Eleonora Kendrick.*

Prov: probably by gift to the sitter's brother-in-law, the Rt. Hon. Reginald Pole-Carew, and then by descent.

The portrait was painted *c.*1810–15, when Miss Kendrick was awarded several prizes by the Society of Arts, and was probably an engagement or wedding present. The artist was appointed Miniature Painter to Princess Elizabeth, and later to William IV.

Lady Sarah (1787–1870), elder daughter of George John, 2nd Earl Spencer and Lady Lavinia Bingham. She m. in 1813, William Henry, 3rd Baron Lyttelton (*see* ANT 24). She was a Lady of the Bedchamber, and Governess to Queen Victoria's children.

ANT/M/3/8

ANT 28

Joseph Pole-Carew

French School (?), *c.*1815

HS facing in a dark blue coat with brass buttons, cream waistcoat, white neckcloth and cravat with gold pin. Pale brown eyes, short curly brown hair, aged about 30. Plain grey background.

Ivory: oval, 61 x 47mm (2$^{1}/_{2}$ x 1$^{7}/_{8}$in). Oval chased ormolu case labelled behind in ink: *Joseph Pole Carew – French School.*

Prov: presumably by descent, through his half-brother.

Possibly painted in Paris after the Restoration, but there is nothing conspicuously French about this miniature.

Joseph (1787–1852), elder son and heir of the Rt. Hon. Reginald Pole-Carew by his first wife, Jemima Yorke. He m. (1) in 1810, Caroline, daughter of John Ellis, elder brother of Lord Seaford; and (2) Mrs Susanna Frances Cadogan, but had only a daughter, Jemima (who m. the Russian, Count Paul de Snasin), by his first marriage, so that on his death, Antony passed to his half-brother, William Henry. The eldest of his four sisters, Charlotte Jemima, married a Frenchman, Comte Alphonse de Morel Champemonte, as her second husband, which might account for the association of this miniature with France.

ANT/M/3/2

ANT 29

Mother and Daughter

Charles Jagger, *c.*1820

The mother TQL to left in a blue and white striped dress and purple cloak, brown eyes, auburn hair, aged about 25 to 30. The child in a white dress with crimson bows, large blue eyes, curly fair auburn hair, aged about 6. Flowers and sea to left, trees in background to right.

Ivory: rectangle, 185 x 160mm ($7^{1}/_{4}$ x $6^{1}/_{4}$in). Gilt-metal rectangular frame with typescript label behind: *Charles Jagger of Bath.* Signed on the reverse: *Painted c.1820.*

Prov: uncertain.

A fine example of Jagger's work of the 1820s, with an interesting background, unlike his usual 'honeycomb'. The names of the sitters are not known, but the mother is possibly Caroline Ellis, who m. Joseph Pole-Carew in 1810, and the child is perhaps their daughter, Jemima (*c.*1812–45), who m. in 1842, Count Paul de Snasin of Russia. The miniature was probably painted in Bath.

ANT/M/1/2

ANT 30

Frances Anne Buller, later Mrs William Henry Pole-Carew

Antonio Bonfigli, *c.*1836

HL seated to left at a looking-glass on a dressing-table, holding roses, in a white dress and blue wrap. Blue eyes, long straight dark brown hair, aged 16. Dark background.

Ivory: rectangle, 112 x 90mm ($4^{3}/_{8}$ x $3^{1}/_{2}$in), signed at right in spidery letters. Rectangular wooden frame with gilt slip and convex glass, and brass label behind engr.: *Frances Anne Buller aetat 16 married W.H. Pole Carew.*

Prov: presumably by descent.

For a slightly later portrait supposedly of the same sitter, *see* ANT 31.

Frances Anne (*c.*1820–1902), second daughter of John Francis Buller of Morval. She m. in 1838, William Henry Pole-Carew (1811–88), who succeeded to Antony on the death of his half-brother, Joseph Pole-Carew (ANT 28), in 1852, and bore him five sons and three daughters.

ANT/M/3/3

ANT 31

Unknown Lady

French School, 1837

HS facing in a yellow and silver striped dress with a brooch at breast, and a fine gold necklace. Hazel eyes, brown hair in ringlets, pink complexion, aged about 20 to 25.

Ivory: oval, 49 x 40mm (2 x $1^{1}/_{8}$in). Oval gilt-metal frame with hair at back, and labelled in ink: *Fanny A. Buller. Artist unknown. Painted in Paris 1837.*

Prov: uncertain.

Despite the inscription on the label on the back, this is neither the same sitter as ANT 30, nor does it show a girl of about 17. It could either be of Fanny (Frances) Buller's eldest sister, Harriet, who m. (1) the Rev. Gerald Pole-Carew (ANT 32) in 1841, and (2) after his death in 1845, the Rev. James Buller Kitson (d.1870), vicar of Morval, in 1849; or it could just possibly depict a daughter of the Rt. Hon. Reginald Pole-Carew's eldest daughter, Charlotte Jemima, by her second marriage to Comte Alphonse de Morel Champemonte, which might at least account for it having been painted in Paris.

ANT/M/3/4

ANT 32

The Rev. Gerald Pole-Carew

Sir William Newton, 1841

HS to left in a red upholstered chair, wearing a dark blue coat, white waistcoat, white dress shirt and bow tie. Light brown eyes, dark brown hair and whiskers, aged 26. Mottled greenish-blue background.

Ivory: rectangle, 105 x 78mm ($4^{1}/_{8}$ x $3^{1}/_{8}$in). Rectangular wooden frame with gilt slip and convex glass, and brass label behind engr.: *Rev. Gerald Pole Carew aetat 26 Pinxt Sir W.J. Newton 1841.*

Prov: presumably by gift and then descent.

Gerald (1815–45), fourth son of the Rt. Hon. Reginald Pole-Carew, and second by his second wife, the Hon. Caroline Lyttelton. He m. in 1841, Harriet, eldest daughter of John Francis Buller of Morval, and eldest sister of Frances Anne (ANT 30), who had m. his elder brother, William Henry, in 1838. Gerald was Vicar of Antony 1840–45. A portrait of him by John King, exh. RA 1843, is at Lanhydrock (the sitter's youngest sister, Juliana, m. Thomas, 1st Baron Robartes of Lanhydrock and Truro in 1839).

ANT/M/3/1

ANT 33

Geraldine Maria Pole-Carew

British School, 1848

WL as a baby, seated on a cushion, wearing a white dress and blue sash, with blue flowers in lap and left hand.

Ivory: oval, 49 x 38mm ($1^{7}/_{8}$ x $1^{1}/_{2}$in). Chased ormolu case with brass label behind engr.: *Geraldine Maria Pole Carew June 1848 aged 14 months.*

Prov: probably commissioned by her parents in 1848, and thence by descent.

A charming but rather crude miniature, probably by an amateur artist.

Geraldine Maria (1847–86), eldest of the three daughters of William Henry Pole-Carew and Frances Anne Buller. She died unmarried.

ANT/M/3/7

ANT 34

Geraldine Maria, Reginald, and Fanny Julia Pole-Carew

Annie Dixon, 1853

WLs in a furnished interior, the girls in white dresses, and the boy in a grey jacket over a blue dress and white petticoats, wearing a grey and blue hat, and holding a bird's nest.

Card: rectangle, 206 x 146mm (8 1/8 x 5 1/4in). Chased metal frame with two labels behind engr.: *Geraldine Maria / Reginald / Fanny Julia / children of William Henry Pole-Carew,* and *Geraldine / Reginald / Julia / Pole-Carew / Pinxt A Dixon / 1853*.

Prov: probably commissioned by the sitters' parents in 1853.

Geraldine Maria (1847–86, *see* ANT 33) was the eldest child of William Henry Pole-Carew and Frances Anne Buller. Reginald (1849–1924, *see* ANT 35) was their eldest son and heir. Fanny Julia (d.1939) was the second of their three daughters.

A chalk drawing of the children's mother, *née* Frances Anne Buller (*see* ANT 30), on the wall behind, looks as if it could have been by George Richmond or Samuel Laurence, but no such drawing is known today.

ANT 35

Major-General Sir Reginald Pole-Carew, as a boy

William Egley, *c.*1853

HS to left as a child, in a blue lace-edged dress. Hazel eyes, fair hair, aged about 4. Sky background.

Ivory: oval, 45 x 40mm (1 3/4 x 1 1/2in) sight size. Oval ormolu frame with typed label behind: *Reginald Pole Carew by Wm Egley*.

Prov: probably commissioned by the sitter's parents in 1853.

There is no preliminary drawing for this miniature in Egley 1839–41, but it was probably painted in 1853 when Reginald was aged 4, at about the same time as ANT 34.

Major-General Sir Reginald Pole-Carew (1849–1924) succeeded his father, William Henry, at Antony in 1888, but his distinguished military career left him little time to enjoy it until his retirement in 1906. He joined the Coldstream Guards as an ensign in 1869. In the Afghan War of 1878–81, he was ADC to General Roberts (ANT 42), who considered 'Polly Carew', as he called him, 'a nice well-plucked fellow', who showed his pluck in the epic march from Kabul to relieve the beleaguered British garrison in Kandahar in 1880. He subsequently fought in Egypt in 1882, in the Second Burma War (whence he brought back a vast bell, still at Antony) in 1886–87, and in the Boer War in 1899–1900. He commanded the Guards Brigade at the Battle of the Modder River in November 1899, following which he was given his own Division (the 11th). He was twice mentioned in dispatches, and given the KCB on his return. Reginald then married Lady Beatrice Butler (ANT 39 & 43), who gave him two sons and two daughters. He became Hon. Colonel of the 5th Battalion of the Duke of Cornwall's Light Infantry in 1909, MP for Bodmin in 1910, Deputy Warden of the Stannaries in 1911, and, having offered his services when the First World War broke out in 1914, served as Inspector-General of the Territorial Forces for a year. Whilst at his Irish seat, Shanbally Castle, he had an addition made to Antony in 1905, in the style of Trerice, but in red brick, so that it looked architecturally more like Pont Street Dutch. Appalled at the sight of it on his return, he remarked that his son would probably have it pulled down – which he did.

ANT/M/3/6

ANT 36

Harriet, Duchess of Sutherland

British School, *c.*1865–70

HS in profile to right, as a marble bust, wearing a cap and ribbons, covered by a lace veil tied in a bow under her chin.

Ivory: oval, 38 x 32mm (1 1/2 x 1 1/4in), sight size. *En camaieu* on a gilt ground. Oval gold locket with rose-cut diamond surround. Written on the back: *Harriet, Duchess of Sutherland, Mistress of the Robes to Queen Victoria at her Coronation, grandmother of Elizabeth Harriet Ormonde, née Grosvenor*.

Lady Harriet Elizabeth Georgiana Howard (1806–68) was the third daughter of George, 6th Earl of Carlisle and Lady Georgiana Cavendish. She m. in 1823, her cousin, George Granville Leveson-Gower, Earl Gower (1786–1861), MP for St. Mawes, who succeeded his father as 2nd Duke of Sutherland in 1833. In the words of the *DNB*: 'He had previously been debarred from matrimony by a romantic attachment for Louise, the unfortunate Queen of Prussia; but the union with Lady Harriet Howard proved one of affection.' It also gave her the status and wealth to become the greatest hostess in the land. The reputed quip of Queen Victoria, to whom she was appointed Mistress of the Robes at her accession in 1837, about her London seat, Stafford (now Lancaster) House, is well known: 'I have come from my house [Buckingham Palace] to your palace.'

The Queen was devoted to the Duchess, and it was Victoria's refusal to part with her and her other Whig ladies that led to the Bedchamber Crisis, when Sir Robert Peel was unable to take over the government from Lord Melbourne in 1839. Victoria spent the first weeks of her widowhood with Harriet as her only companion; and in 1872 she laid the foundation-stone of the memorial to her at Dunrobin Castle (anon. watercolour in the Royal Collections: *cf.* Delia Millar 1995, cat. no. 6218). Illness prevented the Duchess from appearing in public after 1863, but in 1864 she received Garibaldi, whose ardent supporter she had been, even erecting a statue to him (formerly at Cliveden) and giving a reception for him at Chiswick House (which had been lent to her by her brother-in-law in her widowhood). She also attended the great dinner-party given for Garibaldi by her son at Stafford House, her last evening party. A selection of her and her husband's letters was published by their aesthete son, Lord Ronald Gower, as *Stafford House Letters*, in 1891.

The Duchess was painted by many artists, including Lawrence (1827) and Winterhalter (1849; both at Dunrobin Castle; a copy of the latter was given by her to the Queen [who placed it in her bedroom] in 1851, and another copy is at Cliveden [NT]). She was also portrayed in miniature by Mrs. Mee (an

enamel of this, by Henry Bone, is at Arundel Castle), and by an unknown artist around 1830 (Wallace Collection, previously ascribed to Sir William Ross). The present miniature shows her at a more advanced age than any of these, and appears to have been based on a photograph of the posthumous bust of her by Matthew Noble (original plaster, signed and dated 1869, in the National Portrait Gallery: *cf.* Ormond 1973, p.440 & pl.880; marble, exh. RA 1870, at Castle Howard).

Her fifth daughter, Lady Constance Leveson-Gower (also painted by Winterhalter for Queen Victoria, in 1850), married the 1st Duke of Westminster, and was the mother of Lady Elizabeth Harriet Grosvenor, Marchioness of Ormonde (ANT 37-38 & 40).

ANT 37

Lady Elizabeth Harriet Grosvenor, later Marchioness of Ormonde

British School, 1871–72

HS to right in a white dress with blue bow. Hazel eyes, long golden hair with green bow at back, aged 15. Green-grey background, darker to right.

Ivory: oval, 50 x 43mm (2 x 1$^3/_4$in), sight size. Gold frame surrounded with pearls, and topped by a pearled and jewelled marchioness's coronet, with brown hair in the back. Printed label behind: *ELIZABETH H. GROSVENOR AGE 15.*

Prov: probably commissioned by her parents, and thence by descent.

Lady Elizabeth Harriet Grosvenor (1856–1928), eldest daughter of Hugh, 1st Duke of Westminster and his first wife, Lady Constance Leveson-Gower. She m. in 1876, James, 3rd Marquess of Ormonde. Their elder daughter, Lady Beatrice Butler (*see* ANT 39 & 43), m. Sir Reginald Pole-Carew (ANT 35) in 1901. (*See* also ANT 38 & 40).

ANT/M/2/1

ANT 38

Elizabeth Harriet, Marchioness of Ormonde

British School, 1876

HS to left in profile, in a grey dress with narrow white collar and white hat with grey feather. Brown hair, aged 19. Faded sky background.

Ivory: oval, 50 x 40mm (2 x 1$^5/_8$in), sight size. Oval frame with brilliants border, engr. on gold back: *Elizabeth H. Marchioness of Ormonde 1876*, and printed label behind: *ELIZABETH HARRIET ORMONDE NÉE GROSVENOR AGE 19. MARRIED FEB 1876 JAMES EDWARD W.T. MARQUIS OF ORMONDE.*

Prov: presumably by descent.

Painted from a photograph by an artist attached to the photographic studio, probably as an engagement or wedding present. At about the same time this miniature was painted, the Hon. Henry Richard Graves painted whole-length portraits in oils of the sitter and her husband, which are still at Kilkenny Castle (*cf.* Fenlon 2001, nos. 39 & 38, pp.87 & 86, and col. pls. 20 & 19). In hers, a more feathered version of the same hat sits on the pedestal beside her.

For the sitter, *see* ANT 37; and also ANT 40.

ANT/M/2/3

ANT 39

Lady Beatrice Butler, later Pole-Carew

Annie Howard, 1889

See also colour plate 2.

HS facing, head to left, in a white dress. Light blue eyes, long golden hair, aged 13. Faded sky background.

Ivory: oval, 65 x 53mm (2$^1/_2$ x 2$^1/_8$in), sight size, signed lower right: *A.H. / 1889.* Oval gilt locket engr.: *BEATRICE. 1889.*, and with a printed label behind: *BEATRICE BUTLER AGE 13 IN 1889 DAUGHTER OF ELIZABETH HARRIET ORMONDE.*

Prov: probably commissioned by her parents in 1889.

Exh: RA 1890 (1485). Annie Howard also exhibited a portrait of *John Lyttelton, eldest son of Lord Lyttelton*, RA 1889 (1573).

Lady Beatrice Frances Elizabeth Butler (1876–1952), elder daughter of James, 3rd Marquess of Ormonde and Lady Elizabeth Harriet Grosvenor (*see* ANT 37, 38 & 40). She m. in 1901, Sir Reginald Pole-Carew of Antony, and bore him two sons and two daughters. (*See* also ANT 43).

ANT/M/2/4

ANT 40

Elizabeth Harriet, Marchioness of Ormonde

British School, *c.*1890

HS profile to left, looking down, in a white dress. Eyes closed, brown hair tied with a white ribbon, aged about 35. Sky background.

Ivory: rectangle, 102 x 75mm (4 x 3in), sight size. Rectangular gilt frame with jewelled marchioness's coronet, backed with dark red velvet. No label.

Prov: presumably by descent.

A somewhat later likeness of the sitter in ANT 37 & 38, perhaps done with the aid of, rather than directly from, a photograph.

For the sitter, *see* ANT 37.

ANT/M/2/6

ANT 41

Lady Constance Butler

Annie Howard, 1891

HS to left in a white dress. Brown eyes, long golden hair, aged about 12. Faded sky background.

Ivory: oval, 65 x 53mm (2 1/2 x 2 1/8in), sight size, signed lower right: *A.H. 1891*. Gold locket engr.: *CONSTANCE. 1891.*, and inscr. in ink behind: *Constance Mary Butler painted by Miss Howard.*

Prov: probably commissioned by her parents in 1891.

Lady Constance Mary Butler (1879–1949), younger daughter of James, 3rd Marquess of Ormonde and Lady Elizabeth Harriet Grosvenor. She died unmarried.

ANT/M/2/5

ANT 42

Field Marshal Earl Roberts of Kandahar, VC, GCB, KG

Emily Barnard, 1896

HS to left in uniform, three stars (of which, two only partly visible), campaign medals, Victoria Cross, and riband of the Bath. Hazel eyes, grey hair, white moustache and goatee, aged 64. Plain drab background.

Ivory: oval, 81 x 62mm (3 1/4 x 2 1/2in), sight size. Brass frame with tablet behind engr.: *Field Marshal Lord Roberts V.C. – 1896 – Painted by Mrs Barnard.*

Prov: possibly by gift from the sitter.

Adapted from photographs by Lafayette of Dublin (taken when the sitter was Commander-in-Chief Ireland in 1896) and the London Stereoscopic Company.

Sir Frederick Sleigh Roberts (1832–1914), Field Marshal and 1st Earl Roberts, son of General Sir Abraham Roberts. One of the most distinguished soldier sons of Ireland and the Empire (he was born at Cawnpore), Roberts returned to India in 1852, won the VC in the Indian Mutiny in 1858, was appointed CIC India 1885, CIC Ireland 1896, CIC Forces in South Africa 1899, and CIC of the Army from 1900 until the abolition of that office in 1904. He was knighted in 1879, created a baronet in 1881, ennobled in 1892, and created earl and knight of the Garter in 1901.

ANT/M/1/3

ANT 43

Lady Beatrice Pole-Carew

Ethel Webling, *c.*1901

HS to left in profile, looking upwards. Blue eyes, light auburn hair, aged 24. Sky background.

Ivory: oval, 100 x 80mm (4 x 3 1/8in), sight size. Oval blue and white enamel frame with true-love knot on top, and printed label behind: *LADY BEATRICE FRANCIS* [sic] *ELIZABETH BUTLER BORN 28th DECEMBER 1876 / MARRIED GENERAL SIR REGINALD POLE-CAREW K.C.B. 19th FEBRUARY 1901.*

Prov: probably an engagement or wedding present, and thence by descent.

For the sitter, *see* ANT 39.

ANT/M/2/7

ANT 44

Frances, Marchioness of Ormonde

A.C., 1903

TQL seated to right, nearly in profile, in a black dress with white collar and cuffs, black lace mittens and white lace cap. Blue eyes, grey hair, aged 80. Plain grey-brown background.

Ivory: rectangle, 78 x 71mm (3 1/8 x 2 3/4in), sight size, signed lower right: *AC / 1903*. Plain brass frame with spring crest, and printed label behind: *FRANCES JANE, AGE 80 DOWr MARCHIONESS OF ORMONDE (NÉE PAGET) GRANDMOTHER OF BEATRICE POLE CAREW.*

Prov: presumably by descent.

Probably painted from a photograph of *c.*1897.

Frances Jane (1807–1903), daughter of General the Hon. Sir Edward Paget, brother of the 1st Marquess of Anglesey, and his second wife, Lady Harriet Legge. She m. in 1843, John, 2nd Marquess of Ormonde (1808–54), to whom she bore four sons and two daughters. The eldest son James succeeded his father as 3rd Marquess, and was the father of Lady Beatrice Pole-Carew (ANT 39 & 43). During the early years of her marriage (1844–49), she was Lady of the Bedchamber to the Queen Dowager Adelaide.

ANT/M/2/2

ARLINGTON COURT

DEVON

Most of the enormous assortment of curios and bric-à-brac at Arlington Court (for a vivid account of which – including the discovery of Blake's great *Allegory* amongst the 'old rubbish' – see Lees-Milne 1985, pp.182, 212, & 218) was collected by Miss Rosalie Chichester (1865–1949), daughter of Sir Bruce Chichester, 2nd Bt. She lived there for most of her long life, managed the entire estate after her mother's second marriage in 1883, and bequeathed it to the National Trust. The small number of miniatures are (save ARL 9 & 10) family heirlooms, the finest being Sir William Ross's splashy, hedonistic image of Mrs Thomas Chamberlayne (ARL 7). Some of the more interesting include a portrait of Miss Chichester's great-grandfather, Colonel John Palmer Chichester, as a young ensign, attributed to Philip Jean (ARL 2); Mrs James Hamilton Chichester by Anne Mee (ARL 4); Margaret Caroline Chichester, later Mrs Augustus Clevland, attributed to Sir William Newton (ARL 5); a tentatively identified young lady by Emma Kendrick (ARL 6); and a charming watercolour drawing of Miss Chichester herself in some national costume, perhaps a self-portrait (ARL 11). Several earlier miniatures of this branch of the Chichester family (by Cosway, Shelley, and others) are in the Chichester-Constable collection at Burton Constable, East Yorkshire.

Above: the east front
Right: the Morning Room

The main block of Arlington Court itself is a severe Gothic Revival building in dressed ashlar, constructed in 1820 by the Barnstaple architect, Thomas Lee (1794–1834) – a former pupil of Sir John Soane and of David Laing – for Colonel John Chichester (1769–1823; *see* ARL 2). The great triple Drawing Room and the Boudoir survive from this period, but almost all the other rooms, including the spacious Staircase Hall, were remodelled in 1864–65 for Sir Bruce Chichester (1842–81), who also added a new service wing with bedrooms above, which detracts from the purity of Lee's original design. The interiors of the house as they were in Miss Chichester's day are charmingly recalled by a series of slightly naïve watercolours by Miss Chrissy Peters, the former's paid companion, from 1912 to her death in 1939.

ARL 1

Lady in a Black Shawl

British School, *c.*1785–90

HS slightly to right, in a white dress and black shawl. Brown eyes, heavy grey wig, aged about 50. Plain grey background.

Gouache on ivory: circular, 65mm (2½in) diameter, uninscribed. Gilt-metal rim set in the lid of a circular green lacquer snuffbox.

Prov: unknown.

The identity of this lady is unknown. The shape of the wig, and swagger but informal arrangement of her shawl, suggest the late 1780s. To judge by the apparent age of the sitter and date of the miniature, she could conceivably be Mary Chichester (1738–1815), daughter of the executed Jacobite, Major Donald MacDonald. She m. in 1764, as his second wife, John Chichester (1707–83) of Arlington, and bore him two sons – the eldest of whom, Col. John Chichester, succeeded to Arlington – and five daughters, only three of whom survived to adulthood. It is difficult to say whether there is any real resemblance between this woman, apparently in her fifties, and Mary Chichester as painted, looking improbably youthful, in 1780 by 'Sir' George Chalmers, in the three-quarter-length oil at Arlington Court.

If it be Mary Chichester, she is shown when out of the first year of mourning, following the death of her husband in 1783. Once her eldest son had reached his majority, she retired to Bath, where a monument was erected to her in the Roman Catholic Chapel by her two surviving daughters, Mary, Lady (Thomas) Clifford, and Elizabeth, Mrs George Blount. It is now in the Church of the Holy Sacrament, Marton, East Yorkshire.

ARL/V/26

ARL 2

Colonel John Palmer Chichester

Attributed to Philip Jean, *c.*1790

HS to right, in a red coat with white and gold collar, and a full lacy cravat. Light brown eyes, powdered hair in queue, aged about 20. Plain buff background, lit from top left.

Ivory: oval, 58 x 47mm (2¼ x 1⅞in), inscr. on backing paper in ink: *J.P. Chichester / Arlington.* Heavy black and gold Regency commemorative frame with foliage at corners and a cross on three steps at the top.

Prov: by descent.

Colonel John Palmer Chichester (1769–1823), eldest son of John Chichester and Mary MacDonald (ARL 1?), as a young ensign. He joined the Guards in 1786, and later commanded the Cardiganshire Militia. He m. in 1790, as his first wife, Mary-Ann, daughter of George Carey of Torre Abbey, Devon, by whom he had one daughter, Mary-Ann, who m. Thomas Fitzherbert of Norbury and Swynnerton, Staffordshire; as his second wife, in 1793, Agnes Hamilton (ARL 3?), daughter of James Hamilton of Bangour, who bore him four sons and two daughters; and, as his third wife, in 1822, Sophia (d.1847), daughter of Sir Francis Ford, 1st Bt., of Ember Court, Surrey.

Colonel Chichester is known as the builder of two successive houses at Arlington. He died in 1823, following which the miniature was evidently placed in the present funerary frame.

A portrait of his younger brother, Charles Joseph Chichester (1770–1837), of Calverleigh Court, Devon, also attributed to Philip Jean, is at Burton Constable, East Yorkshire.

ARL/P/49

ARL 3

Agnes Hamilton, Mrs John Palmer Chichester (?)

Attributed to Andrew Plimer, *c.*1790

HS to left, in a white lacy low-cut dress and blue sash. Large dark eyes, long powdered hair, aged about 20. Plain grey background.

Ivory: oval, 60 x 49mm (2⅜ x 2in), uninscribed; *Constance* printed in gold on the backing paper. Narrow gilt-bronze frame in the form of a continuous ribbon-and-stick moulding, stamped: *A.F.*

Prov: as ARL 6.

When this miniature was bequeathed to the National Trust for Arlington Court in 1994, it was accessioned as: 'School of Cosway … possibly Mrs Fitzherbert', i.e. as George, Prince of Wales's morganatic wife, Mary Anne Smyth (1756–1837; m.1785), who had previously m. Thomas Fitzherbert (1746–81) of Norbury and Swynnerton, as her second husband; but she bears little resemblance to the formidable aspect of Mrs Fitzherbert. If it was a resemblance of names that led to the confusion, then the sitter might, because of the initials stamped on the frame (which are in fact probably those of its maker) have been thought to be Ann Fitzherbert, i.e. Mary Ann Sophia (1791–1848), the only child of the first marriage of Col. John Palmer Chichester (*see* ARL 2), who m. in 1809, the foregoing Thomas Fitzherbert's nephew, also Thomas (1789–1857), but subsequently lived apart from her husband, in

Paris. Her date of birth makes that impossible.

The costume of the portrait suggests someone coeval with the Prince of Wales's Mrs Fitzherbert. If the inscription in gold on the backing paper is a name, rather than a moral exhortation or motto in French, then the sitter might have been thought to be the first Thomas Fitzherbert's second sister, Constance or Constantia Fitzherbert (d.1813), who m. (1) Joseph Brockholes, *née* Hesketh (d.1782), of Claughton, Lancashire; and (2) Philip Saltmarshe, and died without issue, but, since she would have been born around 1750, the sitter is much too young to have been her, nor is there any good reason why a miniature of her should have been in the possession of the Grantham Bredin descendants of Col. John Palmer Chichester. The person, on the other hand, of whom there is no likeness at Arlington, and who would have been ripe for portrayal around 1790, is Col. Chichester's second wife, Agnes Hamilton (d.1814), daughter of James Hamilton of Bangour, and niece of James Bruce, the great African explorer. Her charms were such that in order to marry her, Col. Chichester recanted his ancestral Roman Catholic faith in Exeter Cathedral, closed the chapel at Arlington, and turned his chaplain adrift.

ARL/P/47

ARL 4

Mary Elizabeth Bateman, Mrs James Hamilton Chichester

Attributed to Anne Mee, *c.*1815–20

HL to right, in a white low-cut frilly dress with broad cream sash, and a double pearl necklace. Light brown eyes, fair hair in curls decked with flowers, aged about 20. Brown and grey scumbled background.

Ivory: rectangle, 105 x 82mm ($4\frac{1}{8}$ x $3\frac{1}{4}$in), uninscribed. Blue leather case lined with blue velvet.

Prov: presumably by gift to Miss Rosalie Chichester.

The picture shows all the characteristics of Mrs Mee's rather sugary portraits of the fashionable ladies admired by the Prince Regent and printed in the *Ladies Monthly Museum*.

The miniature has been traditionally identified as one of the four wives of the Rev. James Hamilton Chichester, Rector of Arlington and builder of the Glebe House, third son of Col. John Palmer Chichester (*see* ARL 2), by his second wife, Agnes Hamilton. She is thus either Mary Elizabeth, daughter of Richard Bateman of Hartington Hall, Derbyshire, whom he m. in 1829, but who died in childbirth in 1830; Louisa, daughter of Robert Willis Blencowe of Dawlish, whom he m. in 1832, but who died after giving birth to a son in 1833; Mary-Anne, daughter of Robert Moyser (*née* Whyte) of Hotham, Yorkshire, whom he m. at Flintham, the seat of her cousin, Thomas Hildyard, in 1836, and who died in 1858; or Mary Ann, daughter of Col. Hildyard of Winestead and Flintham, whom he m. in 1862.

In view of the apparent date of the miniature and age of its sitter, it would seem most likely that it represents the first of these – all the more so in that the son whom she died giving birth to, Captain Frederick Hamilton Chichester (1830–62), retired from service with the Austrian army to die, unmarried, at Arlington, so that a miniature of his mother would be very likely to have remained there.

ARL/D/20

ARL 5

Margaret Caroline Chichester, Mrs Augustus Clevland

Attributed to Sir William Newton, *c.*1820–25

HL to left, in a white silk dress with pointed gold belt, and a blue cloak. Brown eyes, brown hair in ringlets, plaited topknot, and silver and ruby tiara, aged about 20. Red curtain and grey wall background.

Ivory: rectangle, 92 x 70mm ($3\frac{5}{8}$ x $2\frac{3}{4}$in), uninscribed. Rectangular ormolu frame decorated with flowers and foliage.

Prov: presumably by descent from the sitter's father.

The sitter, traditionally just called 'Mrs Clevland', must be Margaret Caroline, second daughter of Col. John Palmer Chichester (*see* ARL 2), but the elder daughter of his second marriage, to Agnes Hamilton. She m. in 1830, Augustus Willett (d.1849) of Tapeley Park, Devon, who took the name of Clevland in accordance with the will of his great-uncle, John Clevland, MP.

Margaret Caroline's date of birth is not given in Sir Alexander Bruce Chichester's *History of the Family of Chichester* (1871), but since her parents married in 1793, and the dates of birth of her three brothers span 1794 to 1798, it does not seem impossible that she could have been born around 1800, thus making her a very plausible sitter for this portrait.

She bore her husband one son, Archibald (1833–55), 'the last of the Clevlands', who died at the Battle of Inkerman, and was commemorated by an obelisk at Tapeley; and two daughters, one of whom, Agnes Hamilton, m. William Langham Christie of Glyndebourne.

ARL/D/19

ARL 6

Mary Bloxsome, Mrs Robert Bruce Chichester (?)

Emma Eleonora Kendrick, *c.*1825–30

HL to right, left hand to cheek, left elbow on a table, in a white dress, pink cloak, double pearl rope over her right shoulder, gold brooch with sapphire and large pearl-drop at bosom, and large gold bracelet on left arm. Light brown eyes, curled and plaited hair piled high on crown, aged about 20 to 25. Architectural background.

Ivory: rectangle, 90 x 70mm (3$^1/_2$ x 2$^3/_4$in), sight size, with a typed label on the back probably recording an inscription on verso: *Emma E. Kendrick pinxit / Duchess Street / Portland Place*. Plain black frame with ormolu inset, and trade label of Chapman Bros., King's Road, to match ARL 8.

Prov: the elder daughter of the sitter, Mary Elizabeth (b.1828); the only son of her second marriage, Edgar Bredin (1868–1934); his son, Hugh Waldine Grantham Bredin (*c.*1901–*c.*1960); bequeathed to the National Trust by his first wife, Lucy Byrd, Mrs Hugh Grantham Bredin, in 1994.

Emma Eleonora Kendrick exh. at Duchess Street from 1821 to 1840. The sitter's hairstyle and clothes suggest a date towards the middle of this period. The miniature came to Arlington with ARL 8, so it is possible that the subject of this miniature is that sitter's wife, Maria, daughter of Henry Warren of Bromley Vale, Essex. She bore Major George Chichester a son and a daughter, before dying at Leghorn (Livorno) in 1840. Given the facts, however, that this is one of the miniatures bequeathed by the widow of a descendant of the youngest brother of George Chichester, the barrister Robert Bruce Chichester, and that it is in no way a pendant to ARL 8, it would seem more likely that – even though not accompanied by any miniature of her husband – it is of Robert Bruce's wife, Mary (d.1868), eldest daughter of Edward Bloxsome of Dursley, Gloucestershire, whom he m. in 1824, and who bore him two sons and two daughters. The elder of these, Mary Elizabeth, m. in 1863, as her second husband, the widower, Major Edgar Grantham Bredin, R.A., to whom she bore a son and a daughter.

ARL/P/48

ARL 7

Amelia Onslow, Mrs Thomas Chamberlayne

Sir William Ross, 1833

See also colour plate 3.

TQL turned to right, facing out, seated in a landscape, in an azure dress with white lace collar, black 'picture' hat topped by a big white bow and with light blue ribbons, resting her left arm on crimson drapery, and holding a pink rose in her right hand. 'Peaches and cream' complexion, with bright pink lips, pale blue eyes, and golden hair in ringlets.

Ivory: rectangle, 146 x 108mm (5$^3/_4$ x 4$^1/_2$in), sight size, uninscribed. Swept ormolu frame with acanthus-leaf corners and crested top, and with a gilt slip.

Prov: presumably by descent.

Amelia (1806/7–98) was one of the daughters of General Denzil Onslow, Grenadier Guards, of Stoughton House, Huntingdon. She m. in 1830, Thomas Chamberlayne, J.P., D.L. (1805–76), of Cranbury Park and Weston Grove, Hampshire, who was pricked for High Sheriff in 1835. They had two sons and four daughters, the third of whom, Rosalie Amelia (d.1908) m. (1) in 1865, Sir Bruce Chichester, 2nd and last Bt., of Arlington, who died in 1881, and (2) in 1883, as his second wife, Sir Arthur Chichester, 8th Bt., of Youlston, who died in 1898. There were no children by her second marriage, and just Miss Rosalie Chichester from her first.

ARL/D/44

ARL 8

Major George Chichester

Italian School (?), 1835

HL facing, head turned to right, in a dark red military uniform, with gold epaulettes and buttons in pairs. Brown eyes, reddish-brown hair and side-whiskers, aged in his 30s. Dark background lit from the left.

Ivory: rectangle, 90 x 70mm (3$^1/_2$ x 2$^3/_4$in), sight size, uninscribed on recto, but with a typed label: *Captain Chichester Rome Oct. 1833 – Rome Sept. 1835*, derived in part from an inscription on verso: *Rome Sept. 1835*. Plain black frame with ormolu inset, trade label of Chapman Bros., King's Road, to match ARL 6.

Prov: as ARL 6.

George Chichester (1797–1876) was the second son of Col. John Palmer Chichester (*see* ARL 2) by his second wife, Agnes Hamilton. He entered the army in 1817; served with the 59th Regiment in Ceylon during the rebellion of 1818–19; became a lieutenant in 1822 and a captain in 1825; was wounded in Sir Stapleton Cotton (later Viscount Combermere)'s successful assault on the Jat fortress of Bharatpur in 1826; and retired with the rank of major in 1832.

The discrepancies of rank and date in the typed label of this miniature, which have caused confusion in the past, are probably due to the facts that the sitter only attained the rank of major on the point of retirement from the army, and that he may have spent a couple of years in Italy following his retirement, before having this miniature painted in Rome. It is by no means certain that it is by an Italian, rather than an itinerant British, miniature-painter.

Major Chichester appears to have remained abroad, as his daughter, Agnes, was born in Geneva in 1837, and his wife, Mary, daughter of Henry Warren of Bromley Vale, Essex, died at Leghorn (Livorno) in 1840.

ARL/P/50

ARL 9

Elizabeth Marchant, Mrs Henry Pratt

British School, *c.*1860

HS facing, in a grey dress with broad black ribbons, and a lace cap tied under her chin with a black bow. Grey eyes, straight fair hair with centre parting, aged about 55 to 60. Sky background.

Ivory: oval, 90 x 72mm (3½ x 2⅞in), uninscribed. Black rectangle frame with acorn hanger; back of the case engr.: *Elizabeth Pratt (1796–1887) Wife of Henry Pratt of Pratshayes (1793–1835) / son of Richard and Mary Pratt / and daughter of William Marchant of Broadway, Littleham and his wife Thomasin, daughter of John Warren.*

Prov: bequeathed to the National Trust by Miss E.H. Pratt of Prattshayes House, nr. Exmouth, in 1960, along with the house and the High Land of Orcombe.

The portrait looks as though it was painted from a photograph of *c.*1860. There is no known connection between the Pratts and the Chichesters of Arlington Court.

ARL/D/74A

ARL 10

Mr Pratt

British School, *c.*1880

HS to right, in a black suit, waistcoat, and bow-tie. Grey eyes, white hair and Newgate fringe, aged about 70. Plain grey background.

Paper: oval, 100 x 76mm (4 x 3in), sight size, uninscribed. Plain brass frame backed with red cloth, inscr. in pencil: *Mr Pratt*.

Prov: bequeathed to the National Trust by Miss E.H. Pratt of Prattshayes House, nr. Exmouth, in 1960, along with the house and the High Land of Orcombe.

The portrait looks as though it was painted from a photograph of *c.*1880. The sitter's identity is uncertain beyond the name on the back. He was possibly the son of Elizabeth Pratt (ARL 9).

ARL/D/74B

ARL 11

Self-Portrait (?)

Attributed to Miss Rosalie Chichester, *c.*1890

WL standing to right on a black and white marble floor, in a peasant costume of white blouse, wide green and red skirt, flat blue hat, and white shoes. Blue eyes, red hair in long plaits, aged about 25.

Watercolour on paper: oval, 90 x 68mm (3½ x 2½in), in an oval chased gilt-metal frame enclosed in a brown leather easel-case.

Prov: uncertain.

The miniature apparently shows Miss Chichester on her travels to the Mediterranean and the Levant. The costume is possibly Madeiran or Portugese; she had drawing lessons from Professor Lanza in Naples in 1877, and the picture, perhaps by herself, may be one mentioned in her diary, still preserved at Arlington. The possibility cannot be excluded, however, that this is a tourist souvenir.

Rosalie (1865–1949), only child of Sir Bruce Chichester, 2nd Bt., and his wife, Rosalie, daughter of Thomas Chamberlayne of Cranbury Park, Hampshire. Her father died in 1881, and when her mother married again in 1883 (to Sir Arthur Chichester, 8th Bt., of Raleigh and Youlston), Miss Chichester took over the management of the Arlington estate, where she spent the rest of her life. She was an inveterate traveller and a compulsive collector, and the house is crammed with a huge collection of objects of every conceivable variety, particularly pictures and models of ships. She bequeathed Arlington Court, its contents, and the entire estate to the National Trust on her death in 1949.

ARL/D/23

ARL 12

Group of Putti

French or British School, 19th century

Five putti sitting on a shell under a tree.

Grisaille on ivory: circular, 35mm (1⅜in) diameter. Set in the lid of a circular *vernis Martin* box, within two chased gold bands.

Prov: unknown.

The box in which this miniature is set appears to date from the nineteenth century, as do the genderless putti themselves. Although *vernis Martin* was a technique first devised in France in the eighteenth century, it was imitated elsewhere in the nineteenth century. The winsomeness of the putti appears more English than French. They do not, however, appear to have been copied from any well-known painting.

ARL/V/41

ARL 13
Queen Marie of Hanover
German School, *c.*1900

HS to left, in a black dress, with a multi-strand pearl necklace and black cap. Hazel eyes, grey hair, aged about 75 to 80.

Ivory: rectangle, 25 x 18mm (1 x 3/4in). Plain silver-gilt frame with crown on top, in a brown leather easel-case.

Prov: presumably by gift from the sitter.

A studio painting from a photograph. The crown surmounting the frame is the royal crown of the United Kingdom, in recognition of the fact that the Hanoverian dynasty had ruled Britain since George I (reigned 1714–27). It was only the application of the Salic Law, which precluded rule and descent through women, that divided Hanover from the United Kingdom when Queen Victoria came to the throne in 1837.

Alexandrine Marie Wilhelmine Katherina Charlotte Therese Henriette Louise Pauline Elizabeth Fredericke Georgine (1818–1907), daughter of Joseph, Duke of Saxe-Altenburg, m. in 1843, George V of Hanover, a cousin of Queen Victoria. He was deposed in 1866, following the Austro-Prussian War, and she was widowed in 1878.

Miss Rosalie Chichester presumably made the acquaintance of the deposed queen on her travels – perhaps at some spa.

ARL/D/34

ARL 14
Adah Holloway, Mrs Henry Chichester
British School, *c.*1910

HS facing, in a low-cut light blue dress, and a gold necklace with brooch. Brown eyes, thick dark wavy hair, aged about 30. Plain sky background.

Ivory: oval, 60 x 45mm (2 3/8 x 1 3/4in). Plain gilt-metal oval frame, backed with yellow velvet.

Prov: presumably by gift to Miss Rosalie Chichester.

Evidently copied from a photograph.

Mrs Henry Chichester, of Hill House, Wincanton, was the daughter of Horatio Holloway (formerly Martelli), of Marchwood Park, Hampshire. She m. in 1876, Henry Chichester (1851–1929), second son of Sir Arthur Chichester, 8th Bt., of Raleigh and Youlston, Devon, who, in 1883, became the second husband of Miss Rosalie Chichester's mother, Rosalie, daughter of Thomas Chamberlayne, of Cranbury Park, Hampshire.

ARL/D/33A

CASTLE DROGO

DEVON

Castle Drogo, which might have been the last thing in absurdity – a granite-hewn, mock-medieval castle, built for a *nouveau riche* grocer and named after the latinised form of Dru, the Norman baron from whom he preposterously claimed descent – is instead one of the most magical properties of the National Trust. Two things are responsible for this: its magnificent site, in a genuinely defensible location between the Chagford Vale and the gorge of the River Teign; and its peerless architect, Sir Edwin Lutyens, then at the height of his powers and fame.

The client was Julius Drewe, who had retired from business a rich man in 1889, only six years after founding the Home and Colonial Stores. Having acquired the site in 1910, he chose Lutyens to be his architect the same year. After several changes of plan, the castle was finally completed in 1925. It was given to the National Trust by Julius Drewe's grandson and great-grandson, Anthony and Christopher Drewe, in 1974.

The entire Drew (later Drewe) family apparently had their portraits painted in miniature in 1906, but for the later-born Frances (CDO 12). The artist was Gordon Chase, who was probably employed as a miniaturist attached to a photographic studio, as his name does not appear in any reference books. He worked with an unusual technique, painting in gouache on discs of ceramic, the general effect being competent, if slightly over-sweet. There are ten of his miniatures in the house.

Mrs Drew(e) also had her portrait painted in 1906 (CDO 11) by Mary Josephine Gibson, who exhibited miniatures at the RA between 1885 and 1908. It may have been she who also painted the later-born youngest child, Frances. A further miniature of the latter is missing from its central position in the group of miniatures framed with that of Julius Drewe.

Left: the entrance tower
Right: Mrs Drewe's bedroom

CDO 1

Julius Charles Drew (later Drewe)

Gordon Chase, 1906

TQL seated to left, holding papers on knee, in a black frock-coat, grey trousers with belt, white waistcoat with gold watch-chain and seal. Black hair and moustache.

Ceramic: oval, 122 x 87mm (4$^3/_4$ x 3$^3/_8$in), signed lower right: *Gordon Chase*. Framed in a leather case with portraits of four of his children (the fifth, in the centre, is missing), one of two groups of miniatures of the Drewe family, painted by Gordon Chase in gouache on discs of ceramic, probably from photographs.

Prov: no doubt commissioned in 1906.

Julius Charles Drew(e) (1856–1931), 3rd son of the Rev. George Smith Drew and his wife, Mary Peek. He founded the Home and Colonial Stores in 1883; m. in 1890, Frances Richardson of Burbage, Derbyshire; acquired the Muriettas' great pile, Wadhurst Park in Sussex, in 1899; began buying land in what he believed to be his ancestral Devon in 1901, by acquiring part of the estate of Broadhembury, formerly that of an unrelated family of Drewes; restored the spelling of his name to 'Drewe' in 1910; and employed Sir Edwin Lutyens to build Castle Drogo, to realise his dream of a suitable ancestral home, between 1910 and 1925, on the glebe land of Drewsteignton, of which his cousin was rector.

DRO/P/35b/5

CDO 2

Frances (Richardson), Mrs Julius Drew (later Drewe)

Gordon Chase, 1906

TQL seated to right in an ornate 'medieval' armchair, wearing a blue dress trimmed with white lace.

Ceramic: oval, 120 x 85mm (4$^3/_4$ x 3$^3/_4$in), signed lower right: *Gordon Chase*. Framed in a hinged leather case with five of her children, the case embossed *CD 1906*. The six portraits were all painted by Gordon Chase in gouache on discs of ceramic, probably from photographs.

Prov: as CDO 1.

Frances (1871–1954), daughter of Thomas and Frances Richardson of Burbage, Derbyshire. She m. in 1890, Julius Drew, and bore him three sons and two daughters, of each of whom there are (or were) a couple of miniatures here. A whole-length portrait of her in the garden at Wadhurst Park, painted by Charles Hardie only four years before, also at Castle Drogo, evokes much better the 'tall, slender, and very beautiful young girl' whom Julius Drew married (*see* also CDO 11).

DRO/P/35a/5

CDO 3

Adrian Drewe

Gordon Chase, 1906 (?)

TQL standing to right as a 14- or 15-year-old boy, in Eton collar.

Ceramic: oval, 80 x 55mm (3$^1/_8$ x 2$^1/_8$in), signed lower left: *Gordon Chase*. Framed in group with CDO 1.

Prov: as CDO 1

Adrian (1891–1917), eldest son of Julius and Frances Drewe. He was a medical research scientist and m. in 1916, Jane Facey, but became a Major in the Royal Garrison Artillery in the First World War, and was killed in Flanders at Ypres. A Memorial Room to him is at Castle Drogo, its contents transferred from a bedroom at Wadhurst Park.

DRO/P/35b/1

CDO 4

Adrian Drewe

Gordon Chase, 1906 (?)

HL turned slightly to the right, facing out, with cheesy grin.

Ceramic: oval, 80 x 55mm (3$^1/_8$ x 2$^1/_8$in). Framed in group with CDO 2.

Prov: as CDO 1.

This is the only case, amongst Gordon Chase's miniatures of the Drewe children, of the second image differing from the first. It would seem likely that the explanation for the duplicates is that each parent wanted a set of miniatures of their spouse and children, but that in this case, husband and wife could not agree as to which photographic image the artist was to work up.

For the sitter, *see* CDO 3.

DRO/P/35a/1

CDO 5

Basil Drewe

Gordon Chase, 1906 (?)

TQL sitting to left holding a book, as an 11- or 12-year-old boy, in an Eton collar.

Ceramic: oval, 80 x 55mm (3$^1/_8$ x 2$^1/_8$in), signed lower right: *Gordon Chase*. Framed in group with CDO 1.

Prov: as CDO 1.

Basil (1894–1974), MC & bar, OBE, KC & QC, 2nd son of Julius and Frances Drewe. Devonshire Regiment 1914–18, RAF 1939–45, barrister, he m. in 1919, Ruth Haselden, daughter of Frank Haselden of Ticehurst, Sussex. She bore him two sons and a daughter. It was their elder son, Anthony (1920–91), who, with the agreement of his son, Christopher (b.1942), gave Castle Drogo to the National Trust in 1974.

DRO/P/35b/2

CDO 6

Basil Drewe

Gordon Chase, 1906 (?)

See also colour plate 5.

Another version of CDO 5, framed in the group with his mother.

Ceramic: oval, 80 x 55mm ($3^{1}/_{8}$ x $2^{1}/_{8}$in), signed lower right: *Gordon Chase*. Framed in group with CDO 2.

Prov: as CDO 1.

For the sitter, *see* CDO 5.

DRO/P/35a/2

CDO 7

Cedric Drewe

Gordon Chase, 1906 (?)

HL slightly to left, as a 9- or 10-year-old boy, in a sailor suit.

Ceramic: oval, 80 x 55mm ($3^{1}/_{8}$ x $2^{1}/_{8}$in). Framed in group with CDO 1.

Prov: as CDO 1.

Cedric (1896–1971), KCVO, MP, 3rd son of Julius and Frances Drewe. RAF 1914–19, MP for South Molton (1924–29) and for Honiton (1931–55), Treasurer to the King's Household (KCVO) 1953. He m. in 1918, Beatrice Newington (1897–1982), who bore him three sons and a daughter. He lived at Broadhembury House, and was patron of the living of Broadhembury, the former seat of an earlier and unrelated family of Drewes.

DRO/P/35b/3

CDO 8

Cedric Drewe

Gordon Chase, 1906 (?)

Another version of CDO 7, framed in the group with his mother.

Ceramic: oval, 80 x 55mm ($3^{1}/_{8}$ x $2^{1}/_{8}$in), signed lower left: *Gordon Chase*. Framed in group with CDO 2.

Prov: as CDO 1.

For the sitter, *see* CDO 7.

DRO/P/35a/3

CDO 9

Mary Drewe

Gordon Chase, 1906 (?)

HL slightly to left, as a 5- or 6-year-old girl, in a frilly white dress with white bow in hair.

Ceramic: oval, 80 x 55mm ($3^{1}/_{8}$ x $2^{1}/_{8}$in), signed lower left: *Gordon Chase*. Framed in group with CDO 1.

Prov: as CDO 1.

Mary (1900–85), eldest daughter of Julius and Frances Drewe. Died unmarried.

DRO/P/35b/4

CDO 10

Mary Drewe

Gordon Chase, 1906 (?)

Another version of CDO 9, framed in the group with her mother.

Ceramic: oval, 80 x 55mm ($3^{1}/_{8}$ x $2^{1}/_{8}$in), signed lower right: *Gordon Chase*. Framed in group with CDO 2.

Prov: as CDO 1.

For the sitter, *see* CDO 9.

DRO/P/35a/4

CDO 11

Frances (Richardson), Mrs Julius Drew (later Drewe)

Mary Josephine Gibson, 1906

HS to right, in a white dress with pink roses. Hazel eyes, thick brown hair, aged about 35. Sky background.

Ivory: oval, 90 x 70mm (3½ x 2¾in), signed mid-right: *M.J. Gibson / 1906*. Gold locket engr. in the sitter's handwriting: *Frances Drew April 4. 1906*, in a hinged red leather frame embossed: *April 4. 1906*.

Prov: as CDO 1.

For the sitter, *see* CDO 2.

It is at first sight curious that this miniature of Frances Drew(e) should apparently have been painted in the same year as Gordon Chase's (CDO 2), but it is so much more appealing than the latter that the sitter may well have insisted on sitting to a second artist, for a proper miniature. Otherwise – since it was done early in the year – one can only suppose that Julius Drew balked at the expense of having his whole family painted twice in this technique.

DRO/P/31a

CDO 12

Frances Drewe

Mary Josephine Gibson (?), *c.* 1909–10 (?)

WL as a 2- or 3-year-old girl in a white dress, pink shoes and sash, with golden curls, holding a bunch of daisies, and standing in a landscape. Sky background.

Ivory: circular: 50mm (2in) diameter, unsigned. Mounted in the centre of the group with her mother. The copy, formerly in the centre of the group with her father, is missing.

Prov: no doubt commissioned in 1909 or 1910.

Frances (1907–81), youngest child of Julius and Frances Drewe. She was married to the Rev. Charles ffolliott Young (1902–78).

It would appear that, when it was decided to have this late-born child painted, Mary Gibson was – unsurprisingly – given the preference over Gordon Chase.

CDO/P/35a/6

KILLERTON
DEVON

The Aclands are possibly the Devon family with the oldest traceable descent (*see* Acland 1981). However, they only began to achieve prominence with Sir John Acland, Kt. (d.1620), who established the family in the south of the county. 'The Great Sir Thomas', 10th Bt. (1787–1871), first gave it a role on the national political stage, with the independent spirit that has characterised it ever since. In 1944, Sir Richard Acland, 15th Bt. (1906–90), founder of the Common Wealth Party, was moved by his political convictions to partly donate to the National Trust much of his ancestral estates of Killerton and Holnicote – at 6,880 hectares one of the most significant transfers of land in its history.

During the late-eighteenth and early-nineteenth centuries, members of the family had themselves painted by some of the greatest painters of the day, including Sir Joshua Reynolds, George Romney and Sir Thomas Lawrence. Yet there are barely any miniatures of the Aclands. It seems improbable that only the few that are included here were ever painted, and one must therefore presume that a case with the finest miniatures was either lost in the fire that ravaged the east side of the house in 1924, or perished in the Exeter blitz in 1940, along with the rest of the furniture that had been put into store when Killerton was given over to schools evacuated from Kent during the Second World War.

The miniatures that have recently been acquired by the National Trust, having previously belonged to Sir John Acland, 16th and present Bt., at the family's dower house, Sprydon, nonetheless include a good example depicting Sir Thomas, 9th Bt., attributable to Samuel Shelley (KIL 1); a fine, not quite matching, pair of Sir Thomas, 10th Bt., and his wife, which will surely be attributable with time (KIL 3 & 4); and two portraits that introduce a new and talented lady amateur, Lady Mary Henrietta Erskine (KIL 5 & 6).

Left: the entrance front
Below: the Dining Room

KIL 1

Sir Thomas Dyke Acland, 9th Bt.

Samuel Shelley, *c.*1790

HS to left, looking out, in a brown coat, white waistcoat, red slip waistcoat, and white cravat. Hazel eyes, powdered wig in queue, aged about 35 to 40.

Ivory: oval, 65 x 52mm (2½ x 2in), sight size, uninscribed. Oval gold frame with dark and light brown hair in glazed reverse.

Prov: Acland Collection, Killerton and Sprydon; until bought by the National Trust by private treaty from Sir John & Lady Acland in 2002, through Timothy Sammons Ltd.

The sitter's apparent age and style of hair and clothes suggest a date of *c.*1790. The traditional attribution to Shelley is reasonable.

Thomas Acland (1752–94), second son of Sir Thomas Acland, 7th Bt. He succeeded his nephew John in 1785 as 9th Bt., and m. in the same year, Henrietta, only daughter of Sir Richard Hoare, 1st Bt., of Barn Elms, and his second wife, Frances Ann Acland, thus bringing much-needed financial support into the Acland family, whose fortunes had been heavily depleted by his father's gambling debts. He was a celebrated Master of Staghounds, preferring to live in the family hunting-boxes at Holnicote and Highercombe, leaving Killerton to be looked after by his agent, John Veitch. In spite of his advantageous marriage, Petherton Park in Somerset – which had come into the family through the marriage in 1721 of Sir Hugh Acland, 6th Bt., to Cecily, daughter and co-heir of Sir Thomas Wroth, 3rd Bt. – had to be sold after his death to pay his debts.

KIL/P/104

KIL 2

Charles I

Samuel Einslie (?), after Van Dyck, *c.*1800

HS to right, head facing, in cuirass, white shirt and collar, and a jewel-bordered red cloak over shoulders; Lesser George of the Garter from the usual blue ribbon round his neck.

Ivory: rectangle, 130 x 110mm (5⅛ x 4¼in), sight size. Heavy gilt-wood frame inscr. on backing paper in a late-nineteenth-century hand, indistinctly in pencil: *King Charles 1st / by Samuel Einslie* [?] */ copy from Van Dyck / at Tuftons* [?]; and, in another hand: *4 / Top right*; and in black felt-tip ink: *82*; and top left of the frame, in old brown ink: *A1*.

Prov: Acland Collection, Killerton and Sprydon; until bought by the National Trust at the sale of chattels by Sir John & Lady Acland, Christie's, 15 May 2002 (141) as 'Manner of Van Dyck'.

The head in this image derives, indirectly perhaps, from the portrait of Charles I in full armour, of which the original is at Arundel Castle (*Van Dyck*, 2004, cat.IV.49; exh. Agnew's, London, 1968, no.44), but treated in rather a fanciful way. The jewelled red cloak over his shoulders is unusual in Charles I's iconography, and does not look contemporary, although he does hold a maroon cloak to his chest in the right-hand view in the celebrated triple portrait in the Royal Collection (Millar, 1963, no.146; *Van Dyck*, 2004, cat.IV.48).

The indistinct pencil note on the reverse suggests the copyist was Samuel Einslie, who exh. miniatures and copies of Old Masters in London from 1795 to 1808. The location of 'Tuftons' is far from obvious. There does not ever seem to have been a house of that name, although it is the family name of the Earls of Thanet. It was perhaps intended to refer to their seat, Hothfield House in Kent, if that was occupied by one of the brothers of Sackville, 9th Earl of Thanet (1769–1825), when he went to live abroad in his latter years. However, the orthography is not clear, and it is possible that the word should be read as 'Tetton', the former seat of the Dykes, which came to the Aclands through the marriage of Elizabeth, daughter and heir of Thomas Dyke, to Sir Thomas Acland, 7th Bt., in 1745, and which was only given up in 1851.

Charles I (1600–49), reigned 1625–1649, when executed.

KIL/P/97

KIL 3

Sir Thomas Dyke Acland, 10th Bt.

British School, *c.*1808

HS facing, head turned slightly to right, in a double-breasted brown coat, blue and white striped waistcoat, and white neckcloth, his right hand inside the coat. Brown eyes, short black hair, smiling expression, aged about 20. Red curtain background.

Ivory: rectangle, 96 x 77mm (3¾ x 3in). Rectangular gilt-metal frame with foliate border, probably a replacement.

Prov: Acland Collection, Killerton and Sprydon; until bought by the National Trust at the sale of chattels by Sir John & Lady Acland, Christie's, 15 May 2002 (143).

The clothes and hair-style suggest a date of 1805–10, and the portrait may have been painted to celebrate the sitter's engagement or his marriage on 7 April 1808. The hand is a good one, but has not yet been identified.

Sir Thomas Dyke Acland (1787–1871), known as 'The Great Sir Thomas', succeeded his father (KIL 1) in 1794. He m. in 1808, Lydia Elizabeth, only daughter of Henry Hoare of Mitcham Grove in Surrey, and third cousin to his mother. He was an active independent-minded liberal Tory MP for Devon or North Devon from 1812 to 1858, and helped found Grillion's dining club in 1813 for MPs of different parties and persuasions. Drawings and engravings of the club's

members now adorn Killerton. The attitude of Sir Thomas's head in this miniature is very similar, though in reverse, to that of the fine whole-length portrait in oils painted by William Owen in 1818, and presented to Lady Acland by his Tory Committee, as consolation for his defeat in the election of that year.

KIL/P/99

KIL 4

Lydia (Hoare), Lady Acland

Attributed to George Sanders or Saunders, *c.*1808

See also colour plate 4.

HS to left, in a lilac overdress with full sleeves and scalloped neck, over a light brown tunic and white slip; pink ribbon and brooch at her breast, and a brown stole over her right shoulder. Blue eyes, red hair swept up and dressed with pearls. Plain brown background.

Ivory: octagon, 120 x 88mm (4¾ x 3½in), sight size. Heavy gilt composition frame, inscr.: *about 1808 / Lady Acland*, and again, on the blue backing paper in black ink: *Lady Acland / about 1808*.

Prov: Acland Collection, Killerton and Sprydon; until bought by the National Trust at the sale of chattels by Sir John & Lady Acland, Christie's, 15 May 2002 (144).

The portrait is not by the same hand as that of her husband (KIL 3), quite apart from the differences in format and framing, and has been attributed by Stephen Lloyd to George Sanders or Saunders (letter of 9 August 2002). It is likely that these two miniatures were engagement or marriage portraits, commissioned separately.

Lydia Elizabeth (1786–1856), only daughter of Henry Hoare of Mitcham Grove in Surrey, head partner of the family bank. She m. in 1808, Sir Thomas Dyke Acland, 10th Bt., and had ten children in eighteen years. She was unusual in accompanying her husband almost everywhere, including to the Congress of Vienna in 1814–15, and to the island of St Kilda in 1812, on which she was reputedly the first lady to land. Between 1834 and 1836 they made a series of voyages – around Britain, to Lisbon, and in the Mediterranean – in *The Lady of St Kilda*, a yacht bought and named after this first visit there. She and her two eldest sons are the subjects of a charming portrait painted by Sir Thomas Lawrence in 1814 (Killerton).

KIL/P/100

KIL 5

John Erskine

Lady Mary Henrietta Erskine, 1812

HS facing, in a brown double-breasted coat (unfinished) and white cravat. Brown eyes, fair hair brushed upwards, aged about 45.

Ivory: rectangle, 95 x 75mm (3¾ x 3in). Heavy rectangular gilt composition frame, signed, inscr. and dated on reverse, under the backing panel: *M.H. Erskine / 1812 / Portrait of John Erskine Esq.*

Prov: Acland Collection, Killerton and Sprydon; until bought by the National Trust at the sale of chattels by Sir John & Lady Acland, Christie's, 15 May 2002 (145a).

Lady Mary Henrietta Erskine (KIL 8), a sister of the sitter, is not generally known as a miniaturist. This miniature is a pair to that of his wife (KIL 6).

John Erskine (*c.*1765–1817) was the younger son of Sir Henry Erskine, 5th Bt., and Janet Wedderburn, and brother of James, 2nd Earl of Rosslyn, who succeeded by special remainder to the titles that had been conferred on their uncle, the Lord Chancellor, Alexander Wedderburn, Baron Loughborough and 1st Earl of Rosslyn. John Erskine, who became Comptroller of Army Accounts, m. in 1802, Mary, third daughter of Sir John Mordaunt, 7th Bt. Their daughter, Mary (KIL 7), m. in 1856, as his second wife, Sir Thomas Dyke Acland, 11th Bt.

KIL/P/101

KIL 6

Mary Mordaunt, Mrs John Erskine

Lady Mary Henrietta Erskine, 1812

HS facing, in a black dress with lace collar, lace stole over her shoulders, and white turban. Brown eyes, smooth dark hair with a jewel at the centre parting, aged about 35 to 40.

Ivory: rectangle, 95 x 75mm (3¾ x 3in). Rectangular gilt composition frame, signed, inscr. and dated on reverse, under the backing panel: *M.H. Erskine / 1812 / Portrait of Mrs / John Erskine*; and in brown ink on the lining paper: *Mrs Erskine / Very like*. Old paper labels printed with: *SIR THOMAS ACLAND* and *1103*.

Prov: Acland Collection, Killerton and Sprydon; until bought by the National Trust at the sale of chattels by Sir John & Lady Acland, Christie's, 15 May 2002 (145b).

The miniature is a pair to that of her husband (KIL 5).

Mary Mordaunt, Mrs John Erskine (*c.*1775–1821) was the third, but eldest married, daughter of Sir John Mordaunt, 7th Bt., MP, LL.D., one of the Grooms of the Bedchamber, and his wife Elizabeth, daughter and co-heir of Thomas Prowse of Axbridge. She m. in 1802, John Erskine, and bore him two daughters (*see* KIL 7), only one of whom survived to adulthood.

KIL/P/102

KIL 7

Miss Charlotte and Miss Mary Erskine

J. Leschallas, 1815

TQLs standing, in white dresses with pink sashes, and coral necklaces; one holding a flower, the other with flowers gathered in her skirt.

Ivory: rectangle, 113 x 105mm (4½ x 4⅛in), sight size. Rectangular gilt composition frame with cut-out paper on reverse, with an old inscription in ink: *Miss Charlotte and / Miss Mary Erskine / by / J. Leschallas 1815 / The former painted from memory under the direction of / Lady Mary Erskine*; and in black felt-tip ink, the large numeral: *79*.

Prov: possibly commissioned by their parents. Acland Collection, Killerton and Sprydon; until bought by the National Trust at the sale of chattels by Sir John & Lady Acland, Christie's, 15 May 2002 (142).

The *pentimenti* around the heads, particularly of the girl on the left, are possibly the result of reducing the heads in size, presumably at Lady Mary Henrietta Erskine's suggestion.

Leschallas exh. portraits and miniatures in London between 1791 and 1823, including a number of copies. This miniature appears to be a concoction, probably painted for the girls' parents after the death of Charlotte, the flowers that they hold being emblematic of mortality. The girl on the right may be Mary, painted from life; and the one on the left, Charlotte, whom Leschallas would have had to paint from her aunt's description, hence the prominent correction to the shape of her head, which the increasing transparency of the overpaint has made visible with time.

The two daughters of John and Mary Erskine: Charlotte (d. as a child) and Mary (d.1892), who m. in 1856, as his second wife, Sir Thomas Acland, 11th Bt. She was a cousin of his first wife, Mary Mordaunt, and nursed the family when the latter and one of her children died of scarlet fever at Tetton in 1851. George Richmond executed two attractive chalk portraits of the couple in the year of their marriage in 1856 (Killerton).

KIL/P/98

KIL 8

Lady Mary Henrietta Erskine

British School, 1818

HS in profile to right, in 'Tudor' costume of sprigged pale yellow dress with a high ruff, and pearl necklace. Grey eyes, fair hair dressed with pearls in an eighteenth-century style, and a pearl ear-drop.

Card: oval, 70 x 55mm (2¾ x 2⅛in). Oval gilt inset within a black rectangular frame inscr. in black ink in a nineteenth-century hand: *Lady Mary Henrietta Erskine / Aged 54 / Died Feb. 16th / 1820*.

Prov: Acland Collection, Killerton and Sprydon; until bought by the National Trust at the sale of chattels by Sir John & Lady Acland, Christie's, 15 May 2002 (145c).

Like KIL 5 and 6, this miniature is probably also by an amateur artist, but it is not a self-portrait, as there are differences in the style and materials of painting to KIL 5 and 6, and it is difficult for anyone to depict themselves in profile.

Lady Mary Henrietta Erskine (1764–1820), only daughter of Sir Henry Erskine, 5th Bt., and sister of John Erskine (KIL 5) and of James, 2nd Earl of Rosslyn, thanks to which she was granted the style, rank and precedence of an earl's daughter in 1801. She was a talented miniaturist, responsible for painting KIL 5 and 6.

KIL/P/103

KILLERTON, DEVON
THE COSTUME COLLECTION

All but one of these miniatures were bequeathed to the National Trust by the creator of most of them, Irene Begbie, Mrs Victor Ellissen (1894–1975). They were left to be shown in the Costume Collection, which was established by Paulise de Bush on the unfurnished upper floor of Killerton in 1973. Although individually unremarkable, Irene Ellissen's miniatures have the interest of showing how the art survived into the mid-twentieth century. It would appear that she simply picked up the other miniatures as examples of her craft.

COS 1
Unknown Gentleman, called the Duc de La Rochefoucauld
Irene (Begbie) Ellissen (?), after Jean Petitot (*c.*1650)

HS to right, in a dark grey jacket and white collar with tassels. Dark brown hair and moustache, brown eyes, and red lips. Stippled brown background, darker to left.

Card: oval, 27 x 24mm (1$^{1}/_{8}$ x 1in), sight size. Oval pinchbeck locket.

Prov: bequeathed to the National Trust by Irene Begbie, Mrs Victor Ellissen, in 1975.

This is a copy of a miniature, in enamel, in the Jones Collection in the Victoria & Albert Museum (*cf. Jones Collection, Part III*, 1923, no.646, p.100 & pl.53). It was known then as a portrait of the great moralist, François VI, duc de La Rochefoucauld (1613–80), but this seems doubtful. It appears to have been thus named because of its close resemblance to the reproduction of another enamel by Petitot, also so called, in the collection of the Queen of Holland (reproduced as the frontispiece to Bourdeau 1895; and in Schäffers-Bodenhausen & Tiethoff-Spliethoff 1993, no.529). However, a more exact engraving by Tony Goutière, after a drawing by Auguste Sandoz of this enamel (reproduced in the un-paginated *Album* published by D.L. Gilbert & J. Gourdault in conjunction with their edition of the *Oeuvres de la Rochefoucauld*, Paris, 1883), not only brings out the difference between the physiognomies of the two sitters, but also makes it clear that, in the Queen of Holland's Petitot, the sitter is – conformably with his rank – wearing armour, with a rich lace collar, whereas the sitter in the Victoria & Albert's Petitot wears a plain civilian's dress and collar.

KIL/PR/1120

COS 2
Mrs Gillespie
Irene (Begbie) Ellissen (?), after George Engleheart (1799?)

HS to right, looking out, in a white dress with frilly edges to collar and neck; light blue ribbon in hair and under collar. Black hair, brown eyes, aged about 20 to 30. Sky background.

Card: oval, 58 x 40 mm (2$^{1}/_{4}$ x 1$^{5}/_{8}$in), sight size. Oval pinchbeck locket.

Prov: bequeathed to the National Trust by Irene Begbie, Mrs Victor Ellissen, in 1975.

The original of this miniature, on ivory, was acquired by the Victoria & Albert Museum in 1904 (Acc.No. 802-1904; *cf.* Long 1930, p.22 & fig.116). It had previously been unknown to George Williamson and Henry Engleheart, when they published *George Engleheart 1750–1829: Miniature Painter to George III* (1902); and either George Engleheart miswrote, or they mistranscribed, an entry under 1799 – a very plausible date for the miniature in the V&A – in his Fee-Book, as '*Mr.* Gillespie' instead of '*Mrs.* Gillespie', or the sitter sat when still unmarried (but there are no 'Misses' in the Fee-Book between 1796 and 1805 inclusive), under her maiden name.

In the absence of any provenance for the V&A's miniature, there can be no telling who this Mrs Gillespie might have been. The one holder of this Scottish name demonstrably in London in

1799 was Annabell (after 1765 – after 1833), fourth daughter of Thomas Taylor, of Taylor's Grange, Co. Dublin, who romantically eloped in 1786 with Cornet (ultimately Major-General) Robert Rollo Gillespie (1766–1814), and who subsequently escaped to Scotland with him after he had killed a man as second in a duel. However, she does not appear to have lived with him after 1796, and the KCB accorded him for his heroic role in the war against Nepal in 1814 was granted (in ignorance of his death) posthumously, on 1 January 1815, so she may never have been styled 'Lady Gillespie'.

KIL/PR/1112

COS 3

Stephen Moore, 2nd Earl Mountcashell

Irene (Begbie) Ellissen, after Charles Robertson (*c.*1800)

HS to right, looking out, in a dark blue topcoat, and white linen shirt and stock. Grey frizzed and powdered hair, brown eyes, aged about 30. Sky background.

Ivory mounted on card: oval, 61 x 48 mm (2³/₈ x 1⁷/₈in), sight size. Oval pinchbeck locket.

Prov: bequeathed to the National Trust by Irene Begbie, Mrs Victor Ellissen, in 1975.

The original of this miniature is in the Salting Collection in the Victoria & Albert Museum (Acc.No. P86-1910; *cf.* Long 1930, p.64 & fig.122; also reproduced as the frontispiece to Sadleir 1924). Another miniature, of the sitter's wife, also attributed to Charles Robertson, was reproduced as the frontispiece to McAleer 1958, when in the collection of a descendant of the younger daughter of her union with 'Tatty'Tighe, Nerina Neri Farina-Cini, of San Marcello. The present copy was presumably made as an exercise, to improve the artist's technique.

Stephen Moore, 2nd Earl Mountcashell (1770–1822), was the eldest son of Stephen, 2nd Viscount Mountcashell, created 1st Earl in 1781, and Lady Helena Rawdon, second daughter of John, 1st Earl of Moira. He m. in 1791, the Hon. Margaret King (1773–1835), eldest daughter of Robert, Viscount Kingsborough (who succeeded his father as 2nd Earl of Kingston in 1797), by whom he had four sons and three daughters. She was a more colourful character than he, who was later described as 'an amiable, rather than a clever man, kind to his children, but careless of their education. Fond of country life, he preferred the retirement of Moore Park [burnt down in 1908] to the social stir of Mount Cashell House … Save for his Continental tour, he does not appear to have been a traveller, and we know that his latter years were devoted principally to improving the methods of agriculture on his Cork property, where he was universally popular' (Sadleir 1924, pp.vi-vii).

His wife, who had been educated by Mary Wollstonecraft as her governess, was a freethinker, republican, and friend of Lord Edward Fitzgerald. Never returning from the above tour, she lived with, and ultimately married, George William 'Tatty' Tighe. In 1814 they settled in Pisa, under their pseudonyms of Mr and Mrs Mason. There, in 1819, she befriended the bizarre *ménage* of Percy Bysshe Shelley; his second wife, Mary Godwin (Mary Wollstonecraft's daughter); and his wife's step-sister, Claire Clairmont, who had recently borne Byron a daughter, Allegra, whom she had to give up to him after their separation. Shelley addressed his poem 'The Sensitive Plant' to 'Mrs Mason'; and after his death and Claire Clairmont's wanderings about Europe, she took the latter in, from 1832 until her own death in 1835 (*cf.* McAleer 1958).

KIL/PR/1119

COS 4

Joseph Brown

British School, *c.*1820–25

HS to right, looking out, in a dark blue jacket with gold buttons, cream-coloured waistcoat, black stock and tie-pin with white collar. Ginger hair, green eyes, aged about 18 to 20. Grey background, lit from the left.

Ivory: oval, 77 x 60mm (3 x 2³/₈in), sight size, inscr. on back: *Joseph Brown Jr. (1802–74) Merchant*. Rectangular gilt wood frame.

Prov: amongst the contents of an inlaid wooden box, donated to the National Trust by Miss Hunter of Tunbridge Wells in 1985.

This is the one miniature in the Costume Collection at Killerton that did not form part of Mrs Ellissen's bequest. No more is known about the sitter than is stated in the inscription on the back, nor whether and how he was related to Miss Hunter. The artist has worked somewhat in the manner of the two leading miniature-painters in Bath in the early nineteenth century, Samson Towgood Roch (1757–1847) and Charles Jagger (*c.*1770–1827).

KIL/PR/1856.5

COS 5
Unknown Young Man
British School, *c.*1830–35

See also colour plate 5.

HS to right, in black coat, white waistcoat and shirt with high collar, and black stock. Fair curly hair parted on his left, blue eyes, aged about 20. Greenish-brown background, darker to left.

Ivory: rectangle, 82 x 65mm (3¼ x 2½in), sight size. Rectangular gold frame decorated with foliage.

Prov: bequeathed to the National Trust by Irene Begbie, Mrs Victor Ellissen, in 1975.

Unlike the previous miniatures, this one appears to be a genuine piece of its period, and not a copy by Irene (Begbie) Ellissen, nor by anyone else. There is nothing to indicate whether the sitter was a forebear of Mrs Ellissen, or whether the miniature is simply one that she had collected.

KIL/PR/1110

COS 6
Unknown Old Lady
German School, *c.*1880–90

HS to right, in a black dress with black velvet facing, white collar, pinkish-white turban, and black earring. Grey hair, hazel eyes, aged 60 to 70. Light brown background.

Porcelain: oval, 80 x 65mm (3⅛ x 2½in), sight size, inscr. on the reverse: *Kunstinstitut fur Porzellan – Malerei Merkel-Heine, Wiesbaden*. Oval patterned gilt bronze locket.

Prov: bequeathed to the National Trust by Irene Begbie, Mrs Victor Ellissen, in 1975.

This miniature, like the previous one, stands out from the rest of Mrs Ellissen's bequest, in not being either an original or a copy by her. There is no clue to the identity of the sitter, who was probably painted from a photograph. Her turban may be a belated reflection in fashion of Queen Victoria's proclamation as Empress of India by Disraeli in 1877. There is nothing specifically to suggest that the sitter was German.

KIL/PR/1118

COS 7
Unknown Old Lady
British School, *c.*1890–1900

HS to right, in an expansive double lace collar over a black dress, and a white lace cap. White and blonde hair, light blue eyes, aged 50 to 60. Sky background.

Ivory: oval, 76 x 61mm (3 x 2⅜in), sight size. Plain pinchbeck locket.

Prov: bequeathed to the National Trust by Irene Begbie, Mrs Victor Ellissen, in 1975.

Although unsigned, this looks like an early work by Irene Begbie. It might therefore be a portrait of her grandmother. However, it is certainly more ambitious than the miniatures by her, and probably dates from as early as *c.*1900, and so may be by her teacher, whose identity is unknown.

KIL/PR/1111

COS 8
Unknown Young Woman
Irene (Begbie) Ellissen, *c.*1925

HS to right, head turned to left, in a low-cut black dress. Ginger hair, light blue eyes, aged about 15 to 20. Sky background.

Ivory: oval, 60 x 48mm (2⅜ x 1⅞in), sight size, signed lower right in black: *I. Begbie*. Oval pinchbeck locket.

Prov: bequeathed to the National Trust by Irene Begbie, Mrs Victor Ellissen, in 1975.

Exh: ?RA 1926, no.901, as *'Head of a Girl'* by Irene Begbie, of 6 Cardigan-road, Richmond Hill, Surrey.

The lack of any identification on the back of this miniature suggests that the sitter was too well known to the artist for her to have affixed one, so it may depict a relative.

KIL/PR/1116

COS 9
Francis Ellissen
Irene (Begbie) Ellissen, 1926

HS slightly to left, looking out, in a cream smock with embroidered collar. Brown hair, hazel eyes, aged about 5 or 6. Sky background.

Ivory: oval, 42 x 35mm (1⅝ x 1⅜in), sight size, signed lower right in black: *I.Begbie*. Oval pinchbeck locket, inscr. on reverse on a paper label: *Francis, son of the artist, by Irene Begbie, 6 Cardigan Rd., Richmond, Surrey. Francis No.2 Exhibited: RA 1926*.

Prov: bequeathed to the National Trust by Irene Begbie, Mrs Victor Ellissen, in 1975.

Exh: RA 1926, no.885, as *'Francis, son of the artist'* by Irene Begbie, of 6 Cardigan-road, Richmond Hill, Surrey.

Francis Ellissen was probably the artist's only child. He appears to have been about five or six years old when this miniature was painted.

KIL/PR/1115

COS 10

Gladys Cooper

Irene (Begbie) Ellissen, 1927

HS slightly to left, head turned to right, in a yellow blouse. Short blonde hair, green eyes, aged 39. Sky background.

Ivory: oval, 59 x 47mm ($2\frac{3}{8}$ x $1\frac{7}{8}$in), sight size, signed lower right in black: *I. Begbie*. Oval pinchbeck locket inscr. on reverse on a paper label: *Miss Irene Begbie (Mrs Victor Ellissen) 6 Cardigan Road, Richmond Hill, Surrey. "Miss Gladys Cooper" No.2. Exhibited: R.A. 1927 129.*

Prov: bequeathed to the National Trust by Irene Begbie, Mrs Victor Ellissen, in 1975.

Exh: RA 1927, No.1049, as *'Miss Gladys Cooper'* by Irene Begbie (Mrs. V. Ellissen), of 6 Cardigan-road, Richmond Hill, Surrey.

In 1927 Gladys Cooper had the starring role in the first play that she put on as actress-manager of the Playhouse Theatre, Somerset Maugham's *The Letter*. By day she was demonstrating her newly-launched range of beauty products. She and her first husband, Hubert Buckmaster ('Buck') had divorced in 1921, and she was not to meet and marry the second of her three husbands, the similarly divorced Sir Neville Pearson, 2nd Bt., until 1928. Nowhere in her own volume of memoirs, *Gladys Cooper* (1931), nor in her grandson Sheridan Morley's biography of her (1979), is there any indication that she knew Irene Begbie Ellissen, let alone that she might have commissioned this miniature from her. It must therefore have been done and exhibited by the artist out of admiration for the sitter, presumably from a press or publicity photograph.

The miniature shows the actress with her hair bobbed. This was the fashion of the day (one of the photographs in her memoirs is captioned 'Myself before the "bobbing" craze'), to which Gladys Cooper inevitably had to succumb, despite Sir Philip Burne-Jones (artist son of the more celebrated Sir Edward) having called her 'the most perfect type of golden-haired loveliness that can be conceived' (*Gladys Cooper*, p.180). She seems to have adopted the style after having her hair cut short for her two winter seasons as Peter Pan, in 1923/4 and 1924/5.

Dame Gladys Cooper (1888–1971) was one of the most admired actresses on the British stage, particularly when she played opposite Gerald du Maurier, and in the plays of Somerset Maugham. She modelled from the age of seven, but made her stage debut in the title role of *Bluebell in Fairyland* at the Theatre Royal, Colchester, in 1905. Her first major critical and social success was in the title role of the revival of Pinero's *The Second Mrs Tanqueray* in 1922. She managed the Playhouse Theatre from 1916 to 1933, initially with Frank Curzon, but on her own after his death in 1927. In 1937 she married her third and last husband, the actor Philip Merivale, and moved with him to California in 1939. However, in spite of making some thirty films between 1940 and 1969, she never made quite the same impact in the cinema as she did on the London stage, on which she played her last role, as Mrs St. Maugham in *The Chalk Garden*, in 1971.

KIL/PR/1117

COS 11

Francis Ellissen

Irene (Begbie) Ellissen, 1955

HL slightly to right, looking out, seated with right arm leaning on a plinth and hands linked, in a kilt, light brown tweed jacket, white shirt and green tie. Dark brown hair, green eyes, aged about 10 to 15. Sky background, with green bush to left.

Ivory: oval, 50 x 38mm (2 x $1\frac{1}{2}$in), sight size, signed lower left in black: *I.B.E.* Oval pinchbeck locket, inscr. on reverse on a paper label: *Mrs Irene Begbie Ellissen. 6 Cardigan Rd., Richmond Hill, Surrey. Francis No.2. Exhibited: R.A. 1955. 44.*

Prov: bequeathed to the National Trust by Irene Begbie, Mrs Victor Ellissen, in 1975.

Exh: RA 1955, No.938, as *'Francis'* by Irene Begbie-Ellissen, of 6 Cardigan-road, Richmond Hill, Surrey.

It would appear that Irene Begbie Ellissen must have painted this miniature of her son from a photograph. One must presume that the sitter either died young, or was perhaps killed in the Second World War, hence this retrospective image; and hence, in the absence of any other heir, her bequest to the National Trust.

KIL/PR/1114

COS 12

Unknown Young Woman

Irene (Begbie) Ellissen, 1960

HS to right, 34 x 26mm ($1\frac{3}{8}$ x 1in), sight size, signed lower left in black: *I.B.E.* Oval pinchbeck locket, inscr. on reverse on a paper label: *Mrs Irene Begbie Ellissen. 6 Cardigan Rd., Richmond Hill, Surrey. Portrait of a Girl. No.2. R.A. 1960.*

Prov: bequeathed to the National Trust by Irene Begbie, Mrs Victor Ellissen, in 1975.

Exh: RA 1960, no.1132 as *'Portrait of a Girl'* by Irene Begbie-Ellissen, of 6 Cardigan-road, Richmond Hill, Surrey.

Perhaps also a relative of the artist, but – unlike the previous miniature – apparently contemporary.

KIL/PR/1113

KNIGHTSHAYES COURT

DEVON

Knightshayes Court might have been one of the most thorough-going High Victorian houses in the country, but its builder, Sir John Heathcoat Amory, 1st Bt. (1829–1914), grandson of the pioneering lace and textile manufacturer, John Heathcoat (1783–1861), suffered from a failure of nerve. Consequently, the interiors of the house that he commissioned William Burges to build him between 1869 and 1874 were only partially realised. The more conventional decorator John Dibblee Crace was chosen in place of Burges to finish them off to his own designs, as was done by 1883. In the twentieth century much even of what he had created disappeared under 'Georgianising' modifications.

These became the backdrop for one of the few important collections of Old Master paintings to be put together in Britain after the Second World War. It was formed by Sir John Heathcoat Amory, 3rd Bt. (1894–1972), almost entirely by purchases from Agnew's, and it was on its account, and for the sake of the gardens created by Sir John and Lady Heathcoat Amory, that the National Trust accepted the bequest of Knightshayes in 1973, at a time when High Victorian architecture and decoration were caviar to the general.

In the event, it is not only for the gardens – which Lady Heathcoat Amory continued to expand and develop up until her death in 1997 – but also for its architecture and interiors, that Knightshayes has since come to be loved by the public. For, whereas the picture collection was diminished by the four finest pictures in it being bequeathed to public galleries by Sir John (*see* KNI 2), and by a number of the attributions to illustrious names not standing up to scholarly scrutiny, the interiors of the house have been enormously enhanced by the uncovering, and – where necessary and feasible – recreation, of the polychrome decorative schemes of Burges and Crace, a process that is still ongoing.

Left: the north front
Right: the Boudoir

KNI 1

Samuel Amory

Alfred Edward Chalon, 1826

See also colour plate 4.

HS to left in a crimson chair, black coat, white shirt with brooch, high white collar. Grey eyes, scanty brown hair and side-whiskers, rosy cheeks. Scumbled drab background.

Ivory: rectangle, 124 x 103mm (4⁷/₈ x 4in), signed with initials, top right corner: *A.E.C.* and inscr. on backing card: *Alfrd Edwd Chalon R.A. London 1826*. Plain rectangular gilt frame.

Prov: presumably by descent, until bequeathed to the National Trust in 1972.

The identification with Samuel Amory is not absolutely certain, but it is plausibly the picture of a man of 42, and the miniature seems compatible with a later portrait of him, in oils, also at Knightshayes.

Samuel Amory (1784–1857), m. Anne, daughter and co-heiress of John Heathcoat. He was a London lawyer and banker (though of Somerset origins), and a partner with his father-in-law, John Heathcoat, in the lace factory that the latter had established in Tiverton in 1816, after the machinery of his Loughborough factory had been wrecked by Luddites. A portrait of him, by Pickersgill – possibly the picture at Knightshayes – was exh. RA 1850 (66).

KNI/P/64

KNI 2

Sir John Heathcoat Amory, 3rd Bt., as a boy

Lucas E. Henrey, 1898

HS slightly to left, as a child aged 4, in white shirt and pale blue tie. Fair hair, grey eyes. Sky background.

Gouache on ivory: oval, 83 x 63mm (3¹/₄ x 2¹/₂in), signed lower left: *Lucas E Henrey 98*. Plain oval gilt-bronze locket.

Prov: probably commissioned by his parents in 1898.

The artist, Lucas Henrey, does not appear in the usual reference books, but seems to have been a skilful miniaturist nevertheless, even though probably working from a photograph.

Major Sir John Heathcoat Amory (1894–1972), succeeded his father as 3rd Baronet in 1931. He was knighted in 1931, pricked for High Sheriff of Devon in 1942, and bequeathed Knightshayes Court to the National Trust at his death in 1972. With his wife, *née* Joyce Wethered, the champion golfer, he created the Garden in the Wood, and amassed a collection of Old Master paintings, at a time when many old families were selling off theirs. These were largely bequeathed to the National Trust with the house, but the four finest were left to other institutions: Lancret's *La Tasse de chocolat* and Van Goyen's *An Estuary with Fishing Boats* to the National Gallery; Poussin's *Mystic Marriage of St Catherine* to the National Gallery of Scotland; and a *Nativity*, now attributed to the Master of the Prado Annunciation, to Birmingham City Art Gallery.

KNI/P/23

LANHYDROCK

CORNWALL

Lanhydrock was the seat of the Robartes family for almost three hundred and fifty years – originally of the Barons Robartes who became Earls of Radnor, but from the early nineteenth century, after inheritance by the Hunts of Mollington, Cheshire, of the Agar-Robartes. They became Barons Robartes of the second creation, before succeeding to the Clifden Viscountcy in the person of Thomas, 2nd Baron, in 1899.

Beautifully situated on the slopes of its park, in the valley of the River Fowey, the appearance of Lanhydrock is slightly deceptive: only the gatehouse, entrance porch, and north (right-hand) wing (containing a library-gallery with superb Jacobean plasterwork) survive from the house begun by Sir Richard Robartes (*c.*1580–1634) after his purchase of the estate in 1620, and completed in the 1640s by his son John (1606–85), created 1st Earl of Radnor in 1679. The rest was rebuilt to harmonise with these, after a disastrous fire had gutted the remainder of the house in 1881.

Gerald, 7th Viscount Clifden (1883–1966) gave the house, park, and woods to the National Trust in 1953, but only included a quarter of the contents, because it was expected that the house would be tenanted. As interest in the Victorian period revived, Lanhydrock was brilliantly refurnished by Michael Trinick, the National Trust's Regional Director for Cornwall, in order to open it to the public. As a result of these facts and the fire of 1881, and because the house has not always passed in the direct male line, the survival of miniatures there is patchy, and it is not always certain whether they are heirlooms or later introductions.

Five miniatures at Lanhydrock are framed together as a group, mounted on brown velvet in a dark red leather case (*see* LAN 1–4 and LAN 6). They were restored in 1979 by the late Jim Murrell of the Victoria and Albert Museum, and his attributions are retained here. There is no information available at the time of writing about their provenance.

Left: the east front
Below: Lady Robartes's Boudoir

LAN 1

Man in a Crimson Robe

Christian Richter, 1718

HL to right, head to left, in a crimson ermine-trimmed robe and knotted lace cravat. Brown eyes, brown full-bottomed wig, pale podgy face, aged about 40. Plain grey background.

Ivory: oval, 69 x 55mm ($2\frac{3}{4}$ x $2\frac{1}{8}$in), signed on back of ivory: *CR 1718* (initials in monogram). Bottom left in frame of five (*see* p.44).

Prov: uncertain.

The sitter's identity is unknown. He is a middle-aged peer in 1718, possibly copied from an oil painting by Kneller or Dahl.

LAN/D/209e

LAN 2

Henry, 3rd Earl of Radnor (?)

French School, *c.*1740

HS to left in red-lined armour, brown fur pelisse and white neckcloth; no orders. Dark blue eyes, powdered hair, stout face, aged 45 to 50. Plain drab background.

Oil on copper: oval, 41 x 34mm ($1\frac{5}{8}$ x $1\frac{3}{8}$in). Top right in frame of five (*see* p.44).

Prov: uncertain.

The identity of the sitter is uncertain. He appears to be a middle-aged man, bearing a slight resemblance to 'Bonny Prince Charlie', but the absence of the ribbon or jewel of the Garter precludes any such identification. Given that this miniature derives from a half-length portrait also at Lanhydrock, it is most plausibly a family portrait. In which case, the most likely candidate is Henry (Robartes), 3rd Earl of Radnor (*c.*1695–1741), of whom there are otherwise only portraits as a child, and who died in France, which would account for the nationality of this miniature.

LAN/D/209a

LAN 3

Lady in a Blue Dress

French School, *c.*1740 (?)

TQL facing, head turned slightly to right, in a blue dress trimmed with brown fur, pink cloak and lace collar. Dark grey eyes, pale bluish complexion, neat powdered hair. Trees to left, cloudy background.

Vellum: circle, 65mm ($2\frac{1}{2}$in) diameter, unfinished watercolour. Centre in frame of five (*see* p.44).

Prov: uncertain.

The sitter's identity is unknown. She appears to be a young lady in *c.*1740, but this miniature may be a later pastiche. If LAN 2 is indeed of Henry, 3rd Earl of Radnor, this might just possibly be of a French mistress of his. Or else, given LAN 2's previous identification as the Young Pretender, it might be another fanciful representation of his supposed 'Diana' in the '45, the quite possibly mythical 'Jenny Cameron' of Lochiel (*cf.* Sharp, 1996, pp.143-46).

LAN/D/209c

LAN 4

Lady in Yellow and Blue

Attributed to Gervase Spencer, *c.*1750

HS to right in a pale yellow dress, blue cloak, and pearl ear-drop. Blue eyes, smooth dark brown hair with pearl clip, pale (faded) face with blue modelling, long neck, aged about 40. Grey scumbled background.

Ivory: oval, 35 x 30mm ($1\frac{3}{8}$ x $1\frac{1}{8}$in). Top left in frame of five (*see* p.44).

Prov: uncertain.

The sitter's identity is unknown. She appears to be a lady aged about 40 in *c.*1745–50, painted in the manner of Gervase Spencer (d.1763). The swan-neck suggests the miniaturist Penelope Carwardine, exh. 1761–72.

LAN/D/209b

LAN 5

Called Lady Georgiana (Howard), Lady Dover

British School, *c.*1780–90

HS to right in a low-cut dress with a blue bow. Grey eyes, reddish-brown hair brushed back on forehead and curls falling on her right shoulder, pale complexion, small mouth, aged about 20. Brown scumbled background.

Watercolour and pencil on paper fixed to wood: rectangle, 85 x 62mm ($3\frac{1}{4}$ x $2\frac{3}{8}$in), inscr. on paper backing in old ink: *The Right Honble Georgiana Agar Ellis. Drawing by Sir Thomas Lawrence P.R.A.* Oblong black wood frame (broken) with acorn suspension.

Prov: uncertain.

In spite of the mid-nineteenth-century inscription on the back, the indifferent quality of the draughtsmanship indicates that Lawrence cannot have been responsible for this miniature which belongs to a previous era – nor is he known ever to have painted one. The identity of the sitter is also very doubtful.

Lady Georgiana Howard (1804–60), daughter of George, 6th Earl of Carlisle and Lady Georgiana Cavendish, daughter of William, 5th Duke of Devonshire, m. in 1822, George James Welbore Agar-Ellis (1797–1833), eldest son of Henry, 2nd Viscount Clifden, created Baron Dover in 1831, but died before succeeding to the Viscountcy (*see* LAN 10). Her portrait in oils was exh. RA 1828 (Garlick, 1989, p.134, No.14).

LAN/D/273

LAN 6

Lady in White

Manner of Andrew Plimer, *c.*1790

HS to left in a white spotted muslin dress and double pearl necklace. Brown eyes, pale complexion, pink hair, aged about 30. Scumbled reddish-brown background. Badly faded.

Ivory: oval, 65 x 54mm ($2^{5}/_{8}$ x $2^{1}/_{8}$in). Bottom right in frame of five (*see* p.44).

Prov: uncertain.

The sitter's identity is uncertain. She appears to be a lady of about 30 depicted in *c.*1790, painted in the manner of Andrew Plimer (1763–1837). The pink hair is an indication of how badly faded this miniature is.

LAN/D/209d

LAN 7

The Hon. Caroline Lyttelton, Mrs Reginald Pole-Carew

Attributed to Elizabeth Paye, Mrs Bryane, *c.*1808

HS to right in a dark grey dress with square-cut lace collar and coral necklace. Large brown eyes, highly coloured complexion, luxuriant black hair with plaited pigtails and brown bandeau. Greenish background.

Ivory: rectangle, 79 x 62mm ($3^{1}/_{8}$ x $2^{1}/_{2}$in), uninscribed. Red leather case.

Prov: by descent.

This is a third version – two others are at Antony (*see* ANT 25-26), and a copy in enamels by Henry Bone is at Hagley Hall – of Elizabeth Paye's miniature of the Hon. Mrs Pole-Carew, whose daughter Juliana m. in 1839, Thomas James Agar-Robartes, later 1st Baron Robartes of Lanhydrock and Truro. It is not easy to decide, without directly juxtaposing the three, whether or not this is an autograph replica.

The Hon. Caroline Lyttelton (1777–1833), daughter of William Henry, 1st Baron Lyttelton, m. in 1808, as his second wife, the Rt. Hon. Reginald Pole-Carew, MP. She was herself an amateur painter in oils, and two copies by her are at Lanhydrock. One is a reduced version of Reynolds's *Hope nursing Love*, which had been acquired by her husband. The other is a gloomy copy of a Tuscan sixteenth-century portrait, inscribed by Caroline Lyttelton herself as '*The Desperate Gentleman*', and claiming that the original was by Leonardo da Vinci!

LAN/D/455

LAN 8

The Hon. Charles Bagenal Agar

British School, *c.*1810

See also colour plate 6.

HS seated to right in a red chair, wearing a black coat, velvet waistcoat, white shirt and bow-tie. Light brown eyes, short fair hair, florid face, bruised look around the eyes, aged about 40. Greenish-brown curtain background.

Ivory: oval, 40 x 34mm ($1^{5}/_{8}$ x $1^{3}/_{8}$in), sight size. Oval gilt chased rim in a blue velvet case (92 x 60mm, $3^{5}/_{8}$ x $2^{3}/_{8}$in) with foliate gilt corner pieces. A lock of fair hair on opposite side.

Prov: by descent.

A distinguished miniature, painted somewhat in the manner of Richard Crosse.

Charles Bagenal Agar (1769–1811), third son of James, 1st Viscount Clifden, was a barrister. He m. in 1804, Anne Maria Hunt (1771–1861), whose portrait by Romney is also at Lanhydrock. She was the sole heir of her great-uncle, Henry, 3rd Earl of Radnor, and it was through this marriage that the Agars came into possession of Lanhydrock. Their son Thomas added the name of Robartes to his own, and was created Baron Robartes in 1869.

LAN/D/453

LAN 9

Girl in a White Dress

Continental School, *c.*1810–20

HS to right, head tilted to left, in a white dress, blue belt and hoop ear-rings. Large blue eyes, pink complexion, brown hair with blue ribbon and flowers, aged about 20. Plain blue background.

Ivory: circle, 40mm ($1^{5}/_{8}$in) diameter, mounted on the lid of a black circular composition patchbox (broken), with dealer's label: *Law, Foulsham & Cole. Guaranteed Genuine 5957.*

Prov: uncertain.

The identity of the sitter is unknown. She appears to be a girl of about 20 in *c.*1810–20, in a 'fancy' picture, rather than a portrait. The indication that the miniature was bought also shows that it is not a family portrait. The miniature is in poor condition.

LAN/D/454

LAN 10

Portrait of a Young Man (possibly Lord Dover)

Attributed to Adam Buck, *c.*1820

HS to left in a blue coat with silver buttons, white waistcoat, high pointed collar, bow-tie and shirt frill. Brown eyes, pale complexion, dark brown curly hair and side-whiskers, aged between 20 and 25. Plain paper background.

Watercolour on paper laid on coarse canvas: rectangle, 100 x 86mm (3⁷/₈ x 3³/₈in), uninscribed. Black and gold mount in gilt frame.

Prov: uncertain.

The identity of the sitter is uncertain; he appears to be a well-dressed young man in *c.*1820, and bears some resemblance to portraits of the young Agar-Ellis by Sanders, Jackson, Lawrence, and others.

The Hon. George James Welbore Agar-Ellis (1797–1833), eldest son of James, 1st Viscount Clifden and Baron Mendip. MP 1818–31, a founding Trustee of the National Gallery, created Baron Dover in 1831, but died before he could succeed his father in the Viscountcy. A miniature of him, by Andrew Robertson, was exh. at the Burlington Fine Arts Club in 1889, lent by Jeffrey Whitehead, and a miniature by William Bate, *c.*1824, was formerly at Serlby Hall, Nottinghamshire (Viscount Galway).

LAN/D/274

LAN 11

***'Le carquois épuisé'* (The empty quiver)**

Dupré after Pierre-Antoine Baudouin, mid-19th century

In a modish bedchamber, a young woman in the process of applying rouge to her cheeks, and still in her *robe de chambre*, looks mockingly down on an apparently exhausted young man sprawled on a sofa. Behind her, on a ledge, is the statuette of Cupid loosing his bow – but without an arrow in it – and with an empty quiver upturned beside him.

Ivory: rectangle, 90 x 70mm (3¹/₂ x 2³/₄in), signed lower right in black: *Dupré*. Rectangular chased metal frame.

Prov: uncertain.

A surprising interloper amongst the sober portraits of this catalogue, and in the severely masculine interiors of Lanhydrock, this miniature has nothing to indicate whether it is indigenous to the house, or was acquired by Michael Trinick. Its character would suggest the latter, since not only is *dix-huitième* French art otherwise absent from Lanhydrock, but its none-too-disguised sexual symbolism seems alien to a house that the 7th Viscount Clifden thought might serve as offices for the Church of England, when he gave it to the National Trust.

Baudouin's original was a gouache that he exhibited in the Salon of 1765 (*cf.* Diderot, 1979, p.136 & pl.46), that was engraved in reverse by N. de Launay, and a version of which was last recorded in the collection of Mortimer Schiff in New York. Mr Schiff's version differs in certain small respects from the image engraved by de Launay, most notably by omitting the quiver that gave the picture its title. It might have been thought that the quiver was an introduction of the engraver, for viewers slow on the uptake, but its presence in the Lanhydrock miniature – which must have been copied from the gouache, and not from the print, since it is the opposite way round to the latter – shows that this was not the case. Although it lacks the full setting of the original, it is thus useful additional evidence to that of the print, to show what that looked like.

The Dupré who made this copy does not feature in the standard works of reference, but two miniature portraits of women in costume of the 1820s and 1830s, similarly just signed *Dupré* or *Dupré Paris*, that were in the Guth sale, Heilbron, Berlin, 17–18 November 1913, lot 38, and in a mixed sale at the Dorotheum, Vienna, 12 December 1978, lot 192 (there identified as a work of the painter Louis Dupré [1789–1837]), respectively, suggest the possible period and locus of his activity.

LAN/D/184

LAN 12

The Hon. Gerald Agar-Robartes, later 7th Viscount Clifden, as a small boy

British School, 1886

TQL seated, facing as a child, in a white dress and blue sash, hands clasped. Brown eyes, brown wavy hair, aged about 3. Sky background.

Ivory (split): oval, 74 x 60mm (2⁷/₈ x 2³/₈in), inscr. in pencil on backing card: *Bassano London 1886*. Oval gilt rim mounted on plum-coloured velvet, in a brown leather case.

Prov: probably commissioned by his parents.

Worked up from a studio photograph by Bassano in 1886, but in very poor condition, ivory broken and paint faded.

Francis Gerald Agar-Robartes (1883–1966), succeeded his father as 7th Viscount Clifden in 1930, and died unmarried. He gave Lanhydrock and many of its contents to the National Trust in 1953.

LAN/D/203b

LAN 13

Girl in a Blue Dress

British School, *c.*1890–1900

TQL seated in a blue dress, holding a teddy-bear. Blue eyes, long fair hair, smiling expression.

Ivory (split): oval, 70 x 58mm (2³/₄ x 2¹/₄in), sight size, delaminating below.

Prov: uncertain.

Based on a studio photograph.

The identity of the sitter is uncertain, but she may be one of the four daughters of Thomas, 6th Viscount Clifden (1844–1930) and Mary Dickinson (1853–1921). A portrait of the Agar-Robartes children, including two of the daughters – Mary Vere (1879–1946) and Julia Caroline Everilda ('Miss Eva', 1880–1969) – hangs on the Teak Staircase at Lanhydrock.

LAN/D/203a

LAN 14

The Madonna della Sedia

Italian School after Raphael, late-19th century

The Madonna HL seated in a chair with a large upright to her right, head in a turban-like white scarf with red stripes, inclined downwards and looking out, wearing a blue dress with a red sleeve and a green shawl with a wide stripe of two rows of lozenges on a dark red ground and narrower stripes of blue dabs on white; brown hair and eyes. The Christ Child on her lap, turned to the left, looking out, starting back from the viewer, dressed in a yellow shift, with brown hair and eyes. John the Baptist behind the Christ Child, with his hands clasped in prayer, turned to the left, in a goatskin, with a stick-cross in the crook of his left arm, with fair hair and blue eyes. The Virgin and St. John have haloes, but the Christ Child has two (out of three) triangular rays. Dark brown background.

Watercolour and bodycolour on porcelain over etched outlines: circle, 89mm ($3^{1}/_{2}$in). In a Florentine leather frame with gilt decoration; label on the back of the frame inscr.: *Mon. Franck / Mont. D.L. Cour 73 / Bruxelles*.

Prov: unknown, but at some point evidently with Monsieur Franck, perhaps a dealer, in Brussels.

The Madonna della Sedia or *della Seggiola* (*'Our Lady of the Seat'*) was painted around 1514 and is first recorded early in the next century in the possession of the Medici, in whose former Pitti Palace in Florence it is now shown.

Already much copied in oils in the eighteenth century (a copy by Prince Hoare is at Stourhead, NT), its popularity resulted in it being looted by Napoleon. Since its return to Italy, it has been copied in every medium, but particularly by the professional miniature painters of the Pitti and the Uffizi. It is not only in scale that such copies diminish the original.

LAN/P/21

LYTES CARY MANOR

SOMERSET

The medieval and sixteenth-century manor house of Lytes Cary was the home of the Lyte family from the thirteenth to the eighteenth century. Its most famous member was the herbalist and antiquarian, Henry Lyte (1529?–1607), who dedicated his *Niewe Herball* to Elizabeth I 'from my poore house at Lytescarie'.

By the twentieth century Lytes Cary had sunk to the status of a neglected farmhouse. It was rescued by Sir Walter Jenner, 2nd Baronet, DSO (1860–1948), son of the eminent Victorian physician, Sir William Jenner (but not connected in any way with the inventor of the vaccination against smallpox, Edward Jenner). He made the property habitable, built a fourth side to the courtyard, laid out a topiary garden in the Elizabethan style, and left the house and much of its contents to the National Trust, including just these two miniatures.

Neither can hold a candle to the most celebrated miniature ever to have been at Lytes Cary, the so-called 'Lyte Jewel': a portrait of James VI & I by Nicholas Hilliard, set in diamonds and enamel. It was given to Henry Lyte's second son, Thomas (1568?–1638), the genealogist, in gratitude for the latter's gift of a calligraphed and illuminated genealogy on vellum, showing James's descent from the mythical founder of Britain, Brut of Troy. Thomas is shown wearing this jewelled miniature, hanging from a ribbon around his neck, in a portrait now in Taunton Castle Museum, whilst the jewel itself, despite the wish of another Thomas Lyte in 1747 that it should always be passed down from daughter to daughter (*cf.* A la Ronde), ultimately became part of the Waddesdon Bequest to the British Museum in 1898.

Above left: the east front
Above right: the Great Parlour

LYT 1

James or Robert? (1789–1877) Stewart

British School, *c.*1810

HS to right in military uniform, sword belt marked with regimental number 18. Short light brown hair, aged about 25.

Sepia on paper: oval, 75 x 57mm (3 x 2¼in), uninscribed. Oval black frame with gilt inset, a label was formerly on the back, in Lady Jenner's hand, stating the sitter's identity.

Prov: presumably by descent to Lady Jenner.

This is an amateur work, possibly derived from an engraving (hence the use of sepia), of an officer in one of the Peninsular War campaigns. It is a gauche version of the kind of miniature that Frederick Buck did in Cork of the numerous young officers embarking from there for the Napoleonic Wars (*cf.* Caffrey, 2000, cat.101).

James Stewart was the elder brother of Flora, Lady Jenner's grandfather, Robert Stewart, of New Scone, Perthshire, a lieutenant in the Perth Rifles Militia, who in 1821 m. Flora Martin, daughter of the Rev. Donald Martin. Their son, Field-Marshal Sir Donald Stewart, 1st Baronet, GCB (1824–1900), rose to be Commander-in-Chief of the British Army in India. In 1847 he m. Marina Dabine (d.1911). Their eldest daughter Flora (d.1921), who m. Sir Walter Jenner, 2nd Baronet (1860–1948) in 1893, inscribed the sitter's identity on the back of the miniature, but it may be questioned whether, given its descent to her, it is of her grandfather rather than of her great-uncle.

LYT/D/42

LYT 2

Lady in White

British School, *c.*1820

HS to right in a white Regency-style dress. Short dark brown hair, cheeks touched with red, aged about 25.

Watercolour on paper: oval, 90 x 73mm (3½ x 2⅞in), uninscribed. Oval embossed gilt-metal frame mounted on a black rectangular board with gilt acorn and oak-leaf hook.

Prov: by descent.

Likewise an amateur work, possibly even by the same hand as LYT 1, but with the extra skill derived from a decade's practice, of a young woman depicted in *c.*1820, whose name has been lost. Despite its differences in technique and framing from the previous miniature, it does not seem impossible that they should be by the same hand: both sitters are given exaggeratedly sharp noses and strangely sharp eyes (though those in the present miniature are more convincingly executed). If that is so, and they were done some years apart, this just could be Flora Martin, around the time of her marriage to Robert Stewart, or the unknown wife of James Stewart.

LYD/D/37

OVERBECK'S

DEVON

Overbeck's is one of the most eccentric properties ever offered to or accepted by the National Trust. It was the creation of the ostensibly conventional research chemist, Otto Overbeck (1860/1–1937), whose working life was spent in the brewing industry in Grimsby. His research into yeasts culminated in the development of a non-alcoholic beer, although its commercial prospects were killed stone dead when the Government – fearful of the potential loss of revenue – imposed a tax on it as if it had contained alcohol. Meanwhile, Overbeck had begun to develop an alarming and completely unscientific device known as the 'electrical rejuvenator'. Writing in the *Daily Graphic* in 1925, at the age of sixty-four, he claimed his invention had 'practically renewed my youth', giving him the mental alertness of a man of thirty, and the 'muscles and skin of a young man'.

In 1928 Otto Overbeck acquired a house called Sharpitor at Salcombe, which had been rebuilt shortly before the First World War by Captain George Medlicott Vereker (1860–1924), grandson of John, 3rd Viscount Gort. There he accumulated, along with his family heirlooms, a gallimaufry of collector's items, ranging from conventional items such as samplers, butterflies, and mementoes of the sea, to curiosities like the polyphon (acquired by Overbeck from a pub, in exchange for a modern gramophone), and an example of Sir Astley Cooper's patent chair to make children sit up straight (from the dame school at Salcombe). Other oddities included a collection of mantraps and handcuffs, one pair of which was worn by the notorious murderer, John Lee of Babbacombe, who escaped hanging because the trap-door thrice failed to open.

Left: Overbeck's with the Salcombe estuary beyond
Below: the Staircase Hall

OVE 1

Dr. Joseph Julian van Overbeck
H. Wykes, *c.* 1880–90

HL facing, in a black topcoat and wearing spectacles; greyish-blue eyes, white hair, moustache, and bushy beard. Stippled light blue background.

Ivory: oval, 95 x 77mm (3¾ x 3in), signed lower left in red: *H. WYKES*. Plain oval pinchbeck locket.

Prov: presumably by descent.

A descendant of Michael van Overbeke, Ambassador from the United Provinces to the Court of St James's (1704–09) during the important period of Anglo-Dutch relations at the time of the War of the Spanish Succession. Van Overbeke paid for his uncle Bonaventura's three-volume *Reliquiae antiquae urbis Romae* (1708), which was dedicated to Queen Anne (her presentation copy is now in the British Library). Dr. Joseph van Overbeck was himself an author, of works of theology, also in Latin. His parents were Dutch and Italian, and before coming to England he was a doctor of theology from the University of Münster, who worked as a researcher in the Vatican until converted to the Protestant faith – possibly through the influence of his wife, Josephine, who was half Prussian and half French. Once in London, he worked mainly as a linguist, whilst maintaining an active interest in religious affairs. He and his wife had daughters and one son, Otto Christoph Joseph Gerhardt Ludwig Overbeck (1860/1–1937), a research chemist in Grimsby until his retirement to Salcombe, where he further developed his bizarre electrical rejuvenator, expounded in *Overbeck's Electronic Theory of Life* (1932), amassed his magpie-like collections, and created the exotic garden at Overbeck's, all of which he bequeathed to the National Trust.

SHA/D/21

ST MICHAEL'S MOUNT

CORNWALL

St Michael's Mount, like its more spectacular and celebrated namesake in Brittany, Mont Saint-Michel, to which it once belonged as a priory, is connected to the mainland by a causeway, and is cut off by the tide twice a day. It has been the seat of the St Aubyns ever since Colonel John St Aubyn (1610–84), who had held it for Parliament since his appointment as Captain the year after its capture from the Royalists in 1646, bought it from Francis Basset, the grandson and heir of Sir Francis Basset, its former defender, in 1659.

However, many of its heirlooms, including miniatures, have since found their way to Pencarrow in Cornwall, because Sir John St Aubyn, 5th Bt. (1758–1839; SMM 18, 20 & 21), died leaving fifteen illegitimate children, but no heir to the baronetcy. The original St Aubyn seat, Clowance, with its contents and the other entailed estates, passed to the Molesworth baronets of Pencarrow, the second son of the 5th of whom had married Catherine, second daughter and co-heir of Sir John St Aubyn, 4th Bt., thus giving rise to the Molesworth-St Aubyns, who eventually came into the Molesworth baronetcy and Pencarrow. St Michael's Mount, by contrast, along with the 5th Baronet's extensive property in Devonport, was inherited by the eldest of his illegitimate sons, James (d.1862), by his second mistress, Juliana Vinicombe (SMM 19 & 22), whom he belatedly married, with a reversion to another of them, Edward (1799–1872). A new baronetcy was conferred on Edward in 1866, whilst his eldest son, John (1829–1908), was raised to the peerage, as the 1st Baron St Levan, in 1887. The 3rd Baron gave St Michael's Mount to the National Trust in 1954, but the family continues to administer it and live there.

Because of its situation, the miniatures at St Michael's Mount need to contend with horrendous climatic conditions, mainly in the form of the prevailing south-west wind, laden with salt water from the English Channel and penetrating even the thick walls of the house; but they have contrived to

Left: St Michael's Mount from the mainland
Below: the Blue Drawing Room

survive manfully. They are contained in three frames hanging in Sir John's Room, and range from a remarkable early seventeenth-century portrait of the heiress, Lady Anne Clifford (SMM 1), to three outstanding enamels by the Cornish artist Henry Bone, of Sir John St Aubyn (SMM 20), his mistress (later wife) Juliana Vinicombe (SMM 22), painted in the late 1790s, and a Miss St Aubyn playing a piano (SMM 24). The original of the latter, a miniature by Samuel Shelley, sadly cannot be traced today. A miniature by the deaf-mute Devon-born artist, Richard Crosse, appears in his sitter-book as 'Lady St Aubyn, 10 guineas' (SMM 16). Between these are a possible Hoskins of about 1640 (SMM 3), an extremely interesting portrait of Charles I wearing an unusually bushy beard (SMM 4), a portrait of Catherine, Lady St Aubyn, perhaps a wedding present of 1725 (SMM 7), and a portrait probably by Jeremiah Meyer (SMM 15). Another miniature of which there is a record, but no longer any trace at St Michael's Mount, is one by William Wood of 1807 or 1808, a portrait of 'Lady St Aubyn of ... about 40, recd by Dr McCullum – only a head – on the Bristol card-board – treganth'd'. This is listed as No.10105 in Wood 1789–1809.

SMM 1

Lady Anne Clifford as Countess of Dorset

Attributed to Peter Oliver, 1620

See also colour plate 5.

HS to right, in a sumptuous white, green and gold dress embroidered with vine leaves and tendrils, diamond and ruby chain, flat goffered ruff, and ear-rings. Brown eyes, pale complexion, light brown hair plaited on top and dressed with diamond and ruby tiara. Plain dark brown background.

Vellum/card: oval, 52 x 40mm (2 x $1\frac{5}{8}$in), sight size, inscr. at right: *Aet. Suae / 30 / 1620*, and with coat of arms top left, of Clifford quartering Vipont, under a countess's coronet.

Prov: uncertain.

Painted in thick opaque colours, very much in the manner of Peter Oliver, who, however, generally signed his works with the letters *PO* in ligature, in gold.

Lady Anne Clifford (1590–1676), b. at Skipton Castle, daughter of George, 3rd Earl of Cumberland and Lady Margaret Russell. She m. (1) in 1609, Richard, 3rd Earl of Dorset, to whom she bore two surviving daughters, and (2) in 1630, as his second wife, Philip, 4th Earl of Pembroke, from whom she separated in 1634. She was educated by the poet, Samuel Daniel, fought tenaciously to retain the enormous Clifford estates, left fragments of a moving diary, and spent the last twenty-five years of her life in her native Westmorland and Cumberland, putting her castles and other buildings into good repair, administering her estates, and creating memorials to her life and her family, including the remarkable Clifford Triptych (formerlyAppleby Castle, now at Abbot Hall, Kendal). This miniature would appear to derive from the undated whole-length of the sitter in the same costume, attributed to Paul van Somer (coll. of Lord Hothfield; *cf.* exh. cat. *Clifford* 1990, no.24; and Spence 1997, pl.22 & colour cover), but the limner has given her more delicate features. A rectangular head-and-shoulders derivative of that, in oils, is, like this, inscribed as of the sitter at the age of 30 in 1620 (Fattorini Collection, Skipton Castle; exh. cat. *cit.*, no.26).

III–5

SMM 2

Sir Thomas Williamson, 1st Bt.

British School, *c.*1635–40

HS slightly to left, in a silver and grey doublet, and falling lace collar. Greenish-grey eyes, pink complexion, very red lips, fair hair in fringe on forehead, fair moustache, aged about 30. Mulberry-coloured background.

Card/vellum: oval, 44 x 35mm ($1\frac{3}{4}$ x $1\frac{3}{8}$in), sight size. Gold locket, the reverse engr. with the sitter's coat of arms and name: *Sir Thomas Williamson, Bar^t.*

Prov: probably introduced by the marriage of Sir John St Aubyn, 4th Bt., to Eliza Wingfield, daughter of William Wingfield of Washington, Co. Durham, and Anne, daughter of Sir William Williamson, 4th Bt. (SMM 12).

Painted in thick opaque colours. The sitter's apparent age and style of clothes suggest a date in the late 1630s, probably a little after he came of age, and 1633, when he married Jane Hussey.

Sir Thomas Williamson (1609–57), created Baronet by Charles I in 1642, 'for fidelity to the King'; m. (1) in 1633, Jane Hussey (d.1642/3), and (2) in 1647, Dionysia Hale. A double portrait of Sir Thomas and his first wife, attributed to Adam de Colone, was sold at Sotheby's, 11 July 1990 (13).

III–7

SMM 3

Lady in Blue (possibly Margaret Lemon)

Style of John Hoskins, *c.*1640–50

HS to left, looking out, in a blue dress, black shawl, large double pearl ear-ring, and pearl necklace. Dark brown eyes, very pale complexion, dark brown hair in ringlets dressed with pearls.

Card/vellum: oval, 60 x 50mm (3³/₈ x 2in), sight size. Crested brass locket.

Prov: uncertain.

The identity of the sitter is uncertain, but she appears to have been a 'Beauty' of the time of Charles I, rather than one of the St Aubyn kin.

The person whose features those of the sitter most resemble – though they seem a little generalised, so that it is hard to judge – are those of Van Dyck's notorious mistress, Margaret Lemon. There is some resemblance to the head of the lost three-quarter-length of her holding flowers, known from the reversed engraving by Wenceslaus Hollar, and from the variant formerly at Strawberry Hill and now at Longleat; but the resemblance to her – if it is indeed she – is even stronger in the *Portrait of a Lady in armour summoned by Cupid* at Blenheim Palace (*Van Dyck*, 2004, cat.IV, 158). The present portrait is bland, however, and the sitter lacks the truculence of either those oils by Van Dyck, or the celebrated miniature of her by Samuel Cooper, dressed as a young cavalier (Fondation Custodia, Paris; exh. cat., Foskett 1974, no.9 & colour cover).

Margaret Lemon (dates unknown) was notorious both for her amours and for her furious jealousy. As to the former, the letter of Hollar's print says: *'Dans l'Ille d'Albion je fus presque adorée, / De mille grands Seigneurs je me vis honorée'*; whilst Van Dyck almost sacrificed his livelihood to the latter, when in an hysterical fit, she tried to bite his thumb off, to prevent him painting any more unchaperoned ladies.

III–3

SMM 4

Charles I

English School, 1648

See also colour plate 5.

HS to left in a black coat, lace collar, blue riband of the Garter. Grey-blue eyes looking to front, long dark brown hair, roundish bushy beard, slightly frowning expression. Plain light blue background.

Oil on metal: oval, 53 x 45mm (2¹/₈ x 1³/₄in), sight size. Faded inscription on back in ink, reputedly copied from an original inscription inside: *Sat for by The King for Sir Bevil Grenville Anno 1642 Dobson pinxit*.

Prov: uncertain.

Lit: Millar 1963; Auerbach and Kingsley Adams 1971, p.246, No.400.

The great question about this miniature is whether the copied inscription can be trusted. Dobson certainly painted Charles I in Oxford between 1642/3 and 1646, but this miniature does not resemble either the unfinished portrait in oils in the Royal Collection (*see* Millar 1963, cat.no.203) or the head-and-shoulders from the Hamilton Palace sale (*see Dobson* 1983–4, cat.no.28). The King also certainly let his beard grow when imprisoned in Carisbrooke Castle, after the dismissal of his barber in February 1648 – but, by that time, both the Royalist commander, Sir Bevil Grenville (1596–1643), and William Dobson (1611–46) were dead, (nor is there any evidence that Charles I grew a full beard any earlier – he had no reason to). Grenville died in the Battle of Lansdowne Hill, with a treasured letter on white silk from Charles I in his pocket, but there is no mention of the King having also sent him a miniature. Nor is there mention of it in his widow's will, which does mention the jewelled miniature of Sir Bevil that is now in the Waddesdon Bequest in the British Museum (*see* Stucley 1983, pp.148-9 & pls. 3a & b). Finally, not only is there no suggestion of Dobson's style when painting on a normal scale in oils in this miniature, but there is also no evidence that he was either taught to paint miniatures, or that he ever practised the art.

Another example of this interesting portrait of Charles I is in Lord Salisbury's collection at Hatfield House, also painted in oils on copper, but unattributed (*see* Auerbach & Kingsley Adams 1971, cat.no.400). Edward Bower's portrait in oils of Charles I during his trial in January 1648–9 – one of the four original versions of which is at Antony – also shows him with a substantial, but neatly trimmed, beard (*see* Millar 1963, cat.no.208 and *Charles I* 1972, cat.no.175). It is uncertain whether the King's beard was trimmed for his trial, or whether Bower just did so in his portrait, to lend Charles greater dignity. In which case, this miniature and the one at Hatfield were probably done from a drawing that might have been made at any time between the monarch's arrival at Windsor from Carisbrooke and Hurst Castles on 23 December 1648, and his execution on 30 January 1649.

Charles I (1600–49), reigned 1625–49.

III–4

SMM 5

Lord Edward Howard

Attributed to Nicholas Dixon, 1683

HL to right in armour and full lace cravat. Brown eyes, long brown wig, pale complexion, double chin, aged 43. Yellowish-brown background.

Card: oval, 58 x 47mm (2¼ x 1⅞in), sight size; contemporary inscr. on the card backing in brown ink: *1683 / December 4th / Edward Howard / third brother to / Henry Howard / now Duke of Norfolk / Etatis suo / 43*. Pinchbeck frame.

Prov: uncertain.

The traditional attribution to Dixon is uncertain, as the sitter does not have the characteristic 'Dixon' eyes and reddish-brown complexion.

Lord Edward Howard (b.*c.*1640), sixth but third surviving son of Henry Frederick, Earl of Arundel, and younger brother of the 5th and 6th Dukes of Norfolk. He was granted the courtesy title 'Lord', though only the son of an earl, because the dukedom – which had been forfeited when his great-great-grandfather, the 4th Duke, was attainted for high treason and beheaded in 1572 – was restored to the 5th Duke by Act of Parliament in 1660.

It is not clear why there should be a portrait of this sitter at St Michael's Mount.

III–1

SMM 6

Portrait of a Man in Blue

Attributed to Charles Boit, *c.*1720

HS to left in a blue coat, white neckcloth and cravat. Blue eyes, long light brown hair, aged about 25. Plain yellowish-brown background.

Enamel: oval, 52 x 42mm (2 x 1¾in), sight size. Heavy rectangular giltwood frame backed with green baize. Repaired by Sotheby's in 1993.

The identity of the sitter is unknown. He appears to be a young man in *c.*1720.

II–7

SMM 7

Catherine (Morice), Lady St Aubyn

British School, 19th century, after an original of *c.*1725

HS slightly to left, in a low-cut blue dress. Green-blue eyes, long fair hair. Light blue background, with hatching to left.

Ivory: oval, 44 x 35mm (1¾ x 1⅜in), sight size. Pinchbeck locket engr. on back: *Catherine Morice ELDEST DAUGHTER AND COHEIRESS of Sir Nicholas Morice, Bart. MARRIED 1725, Sir John St Aubyn, Bart. DIED June 16 1746. HER DAUGHTER Barbara St Aubyn MARRIED June 22 1762 Sir John Molesworth, Bart.*

Prov: presumably by descent.

This is a later copy of a signed miniature by Bernard Lens that is now at Pencarrow, and a companion to SMM 8.

Catherine (*c.*1700–1740 or 1746), elder daughter of Sir Nicholas Morice, 2nd Baronet. She m. in 1725, Sir John St Aubyn, 3rd Baronet. Catherine and her sister, Barbara (SMM 8), who were also grand-daughters of Thomas, 8th Earl of Pembroke, brought the Morice estates, except Werrington (*see* TYN 10), to their St Aubyn and Molesworth husbands, whose families were linked by subsequent marriages.

III–6

SMM 8

Barbara (Morice), Lady Molesworth

British School, 19th century, after a John Vanderbank of *c.*1730

HS to right in a once-blue dress. Grey-green eyes, pink complexion, long gingerish-brown hair over shoulders, pearl hair-clasp and pearl ear-drops. Drab greenish background (damaged by damp).

Ivory: oval, 45 x 37mm (1¾ x 1½in), sight size. Pinchbeck locket engr. on back: *Barbara Morice 2nd DAUGHTER AND COHEIRESS OF Sir Nicholas Morice Bart BORN 1711 MARRIED 1728 TO Sir John Molesworth Bart DIED May 17th 1735.*

Prov: presumably by descent.

This is a later copy of a miniature at Pencarrow ascribed to William Prewett, that was itself copied from one of the no less than three portraits of this sitter by Vanderbank that are also at Pencarrow (Courtauld Photographic Survey list, nos.65 or 66), but giving the sitter lighter hair. The miniature is by the same hand as SMM 7, and is not of high quality.

Barbara (1711–35), younger daughter of Sir Nicholas Morice, 2nd Baronet, and sister of Catherine, Lady St Aubyn (*see* SMM 7). She m. in 1728, Sir John Molesworth, 4th Baronet of Pencarrow.

II–12

SMM 9

Lady Lucy Morice

Jacques-Antoine Arlaud, *c.*1731

HS slightly to left in a low-cut blue dress. Blue eyes, long fair hair with a tress over her left shoulder, pale pink complexion, smiling expression.

Ivory/card: oval, 54 x 45mm (2⅛ x 1¾in), sight size; signed lower right in black paint in monogram: *JAA*. Brass frame, with ribbon-and-stick moulding on fore-edge, inscribed on the back: *Lady Lucy Morice*.

Prov: probably by descent (*see* below).

After an anonymous miniature at Pencarrow, that was probably painted in the early 1730s, and perhaps an engagement or marriage portrait.

Lucy (d.1738/9), daughter of Thomas, 1st Marquess of Wharton and his second wife, the Hon. Lucy Loftus. She m. in 1731, as his first wife, Sir William Morice, 3rd and last Baronet (*c.*1707–49/50); he appears to have divorced her. She went to live in Chelsea, but died at Bath. When he died, his unsettled estates devolved on the St Aubyn and Molesworth families (his father, Sir Nicholas Morice, 2nd Bt., had otherwise had only two daughters: Catherine, the elder, who m. Sir John St Aubyn, 3rd Bt.; and Barbara, who m. Sir John Molesworth, 4th Bt.), which is doubtless how this miniature came to be at St Michael's Mount.

II–2

SMM 10

Lady in a Blue Dress

British School, after an original of *c.*1740

HL to right, head turned to face, in a low-cut blue dress with a white stomacher. Brown eyes, short black hair, pale complexion, and matronly figure. Stippled grey background.

Ivory: oval, 48 x 38mm (1 7/8 x 1 1/2in), sight size. Pinchbeck case.

Prov: uncertain.

A copy, not of very high quality, of a portrait perhaps by Jervas or Richardson. The identity of the sitter is not known; she appears to be a middle-aged lady depicted *c.*1740, possibly one of the sisters of Sir John St Aubyn, 3rd Baronet.

II–1

SMM 11

Young Man in a Pink Coat

British School, *c.*1760 (?)

HS to right in a once-pink coat trimmed with white lace. Light grey eyes, long grey powdered hair in ringlets falling over shoulders, colours very faded. Plain grey background.

Ivory: oval, 38 x 31mm (1 1/2 x 1 1/4in), sight size. Pinchbeck case.

Prov: uncertain.

The identity of the sitter is not known; he appears to be a rather fancifully dressed young man in the 1760s, of the same generation as Sir John St Aubyn, 4th Baronet; but the handling is such as to suggest the possibility that this is a later pastiche.

II–3

SMM 12

Anne (Williamson), Mrs William Wingfield

Attributed to Ozias Humphry, 1768

HS to left in a white lace dress, white lace cap tied under the chin, and a pink rose at the bosom. Dark eyes, black hair, pale pink complexion. Plain grey background.

Ivory: oval, 34 x 29mm (1 3/8 x 1 1/8in), sight size, in a gold locket engr. on reverse: *Mrs Wingfield / July 1768.*

Prov: presumably by descent.

This miniature is characteristic of Humphry's work, but does not appear in Williamson 1918.

An oval head-and-shoulders portrait in oils of the sitter, similarly attired, described as 'School of Alan Ramsay', was in the collection of Col. F.J.B. Wingfield Digby, when exhibited in *Pictures from Midland Houses* at the Birmingham City Art Gallery in 1938 (no.99).

Anne, daughter of Sir William Williamson, 4th Baronet (*see* SMM 2). She m. William Wingfield of Washington, Co. Durham, and was the mother of Elizabeth, Lady St Aubyn (SMM 16).

III–2

SMM 13

Young Man in a Red Coat

British School, *c.*1770 (?)

HS to right in a once-red coat with brass buttons, white neckcloth, and lace shirt-frill. Grey eyes, pale complexion, powdered wig tied by black ribbon at the back. Dark blue background.

Ivory: oval, 44 x 35mm (1 3/4 x 1 3/8in), sight size. Pinchbeck locket with green silk backing.

Prov: uncertain.

Perhaps originally the pendant of SMM 25. The identity of the sitter is not known; he appears to be a young man in *c.*1770, of the same generation as Sir John St Aubyn, 4th Baronet. But, as with SMM 11, the handling – and, in this case, the over-dramatised eyes, which look like those in an illustration to one of Baroness Orczy's novels – suggest a later pastiche.

I–2

SMM 14

Lady in a Lilac Dress

Attributed to Richard Crosse, *c.*1775

HS facing, head turned to left, in a lilac-coloured dress trimmed with white lace. Brown eyes, florid complexion, powdered hair on crown and dressed with pearls, with a lock falling over her right shoulder. Plain grey background, darker to left.

Enamel: oval, 56 x 46mm (2 1/4 x 1 3/4in), sight size. Pinchbeck case.

Prov: uncertain.

The identity of the sitter is uncertain; she appears to be a well-dressed lady of the 1770s, of the same generation as Sir John St Aubyn, 4th Baronet.

II–10

SMM 15

Lady in Blue

Attributed to Jeremiah Meyer, *c.*1775

See also colour plate 5.

HS to left in a once-blue low-cut dress. Blue eyes, pale complexion modelled with blue-grey strokes, long luxuriant black hair falling over her right shoulder. Plain greenish-grey background, darker to left.

Ivory: oval, 42 x 34mm ($1\frac{5}{8}$ x $1\frac{3}{8}$in), sight size. Pinchbeck case.

Prov: uncertain.

This miniature is traditionally attributed to Richard Crosse, but the style is nearer to Jeremiah Meyer. The identity of the sitter is unknown; she appears to be a well-dressed young lady in *c.*1775–80, so is possibly one of the four sisters of Sir John St Aubyn, 5th Baronet: Elizabeth (b.1757; m. in 1790, Humphrey Prideaux); Catherine (b.1760; m. in 1790, the Rev. John Molesworth) – the least probable: *see* SMM 24; Dorothy (b.1760; m. in 1787, Sir Thomas Barrett-Lennard); or Anne (b.1762; m. Robert White).

II–5

SMM 16

Elizabeth (Wingfield), Lady St Aubyn

Richard Crosse, 1778

HS to left in a low-cut white dress edged with gold, and a blue bow at her bosom. Dark brown eyes, pale (faded) complexion, luxuriant black hair, high on top, a lock falling over her right shoulder. Plain blue-grey background.

Ivory: oval, 51 x 42mm (2 x $1\frac{3}{4}$in), sight size. Pinchbeck locket.

Prov: uncertain, but possibly commissioned by the sitter in 1778.

Lit: Long 1929, p.69.

The identity of the sitter is not absolutely certain, but the entry in Crosse's ledger for 1 June 1778, 'Lady St Aubyn for her picture, 10 guineas', makes it a very likely possibility. The inside of the locket is inscr.: *W.H. Jan 1908.* It has not proved possible to identify 'W.H.'.

Elizabeth (d.1796), daughter of William Wingfield, of Washington, Co. Durham, and his wife Anne, daughter of Sir William Williamson, 4th Baronet (SMM 12). She m. (1) in 1756, Sir John St Aubyn, 4th Baronet (d.1772), and (2) in 1782, John Baker of Orsett, Essex.

II–11

SMM 17

Young Lady in a White Cap

James Nixon, *c.*1785–95

HS to right, head slightly tilted, in a white shift, black cloak, and elaborate white lace cap. Blue eyes, luxuriant auburn hair, pale complexion. Grey-green background with a streak of copper.

Ivory: oval, 66 x 52mm ($2\frac{5}{8}$ x $2\frac{1}{8}$in), sight size. Pinchbeck frame.

Prov: uncertain.

The sitter in this miniature is again unknown, but the voluminous headgear suggests a date in the late 1780s, so that she could be another of the sisters of Sir John St Aubyn, 5th Baronet (*see* SMM 15), portrayed at a rather later date.

II–4

SMM 18

Sir John St Aubyn, 5th Bt., M.P., F.S.A.

Anne Phyllis Jessup, Lady Beechey (?), *c.*1795

HS to right in a royal blue coat with collar high at back, and voluminous white stock knotted with a bow, with bold white highlights. Grey eyes, pink complexion, powdered wig in queue. Plain grey hatched background.

Ivory: oval, 66 x 53mm ($2\frac{5}{8}$ x $2\frac{1}{8}$in), sight size. Pinchbeck locket with plait of light brown hair.

Prov: presumably by descent.

This is the original of the enamel by Henry Bone (SMM 20). The drawing for that (now in the NPG) is inscribed as being of 'Sr. J. St. Aubyn after Beechey, 1795'. There is indeed a fine portrait in oils of the 5th Baronet by Sir William Beechey (1753–1839) at Pencarrow, but it does not resemble this miniature. Sir William had, moreover, begun by painting small-scale portraits in oils, not miniatures, and had moved on to portraits on the scale of life by the time of his return to London from his sojourn in Norwich between 1782 and 1787. The only plausible conclusion must then be that the 'Beechey' referred to is his second wife, Anne Phyllis Jessup, whom he married in 1793, and who was a miniature painter.

John (1758–1839), elder, and only surviving, son of Sir John St Aubyn, 4th Baronet, whom he succeeded as 5th Baronet in 1772. He had two mistresses and fifteen illegitimate children, before finally marrying Juliana Vinicombe (1769–1856) in 1822. He was a lover of science, a keen mineralogist, a friend of the Cornish artist, John Opie, and an enthusiastic and discriminating collector of prints and books, which were dispersed in twenty-nine days of sales after his and his widow's deaths. For Sir John was also extravagant, having already been sued for debts incurred when he was at Westminster School, aged seventeen, and having incumbered his property with £130,000 of marriage portions for his children. Other portraits of him are by J.S.C. Schaak (*c.*1765, at Pencarrow); a three-quarter-length in oils by Nathaniel Hone (1775, at St Michael's Mount); a miniature by Joseph Saunders (*c.*1780, in the collection of Captain St John McClosky); Sir Joshua Reynolds (1786, at Pencarrow, with a copy by Opie at St Michael's Mount); Sir William Beechey (*c.*1790, at Pencarrow); and Henry Edridge (*c.*1815, collection of J.M. St Aubyn). An enamel miniature of him, by Jacques Thouron, *c.*1780, was sold at Christie's, 16 December 1980 (219).

I–5

SMM 19

Juliana Vinicombe, later Lady St Aubyn

British School, *c.*1795

HL to right in a white dress tied below the bosom, turban, and necklace of four rows of pearls. Grey eyes, pink complexion, long powdered hair over both shoulders.

Ivory: oval, 77 x 65mm (3 x $2^{5}/_{8}$in), sight size; a plait of dark brown hair in reverse of pinchbeck locket, engraved on the rim: *Juliana Lady St Aubyn*.

Prov: presumably by descent.

The sitter is shown as a young lady in the mid-1790s. Although the miniature is a little larger than SMM 18, it would appear to be by the same hand, and the sitter's hair at the back is plaited in exactly the same fashion. It might at first sight seem surprising that she should be the same sitter as in SMM 22, but that is because she is still wearing her hair powdered here.

Juliana Vinicombe (1769–1856) was the daughter of a farmer or small landowner from Marazion (the village linked to St Michael's Mount by a tidally-submerged stone causeway), who became Sir John's second mistress. She bore him eight or nine children, but only when they were grown up did he marry her, in 1822. St Michael's Mount and the baronet's property at Devonport were left to the eldest surviving of them, James (d.1862), with a reversion to the fourth son, Edward (1799–1872) and his descendants. Edward was made a baronet in 1866, and his eldest son, John (1829–1908), was raised to the peerage in 1887, as the 1st Baron St Levan.

II–6

SMM 20

Sir John St Aubyn, 5th Bt., MP, FSA

Henry Bone, 1795

HS to right in a dark blue coat with collar high at the back, white neckcloth, and voluminous white bow-tie. Blue eyes, grey wig in queue, fresh young complexion, serious expression. Plain grey background.

Enamel: oval, 67 x 55mm ($2^{5}/_{8}$ x $2^{1}/_{8}$in), sight size, signed lower right: *HBone*, and inscr. on turquoise counter-enamel (under glass and surrounded by a fine plait of light brown hair): *Sr John St Aubyn / Cornwall / Henry Bone ft. / Jany 179*[?], the last numeral probably 5. Plain brass locket.

Prov: probably commissioned by the sitter *c.*1794.

Exh: RA 1798 (878); Truro 1951 (6).

Lit: Farington 1978–84, entry for 31 March 1811; Hartley 1977, pp.31 ff; St Aubyn 1978, p.25.

For the sitter, *see* SMM 18.

Henry Bone's preliminary drawing for this enamel, squared, numbered, and inscr.: *'Sr J. St Aubyn after Beechey 1795'*, is in the NPG library (Bone Drawings III.2b). The original miniature, by Sir William Beechey's second wife, Anne Phyllis Jessup, is also on St Michael's Mount (SMM 18).

I–4

SMM 21

Sir John St Aubyn, 5th Bt., MP, FSA

Attributed to Charles Shirreff, *c.*1795

HS to left in a black coat with white lapels, and white neckcloth knotted into a small bow. Pale grey eyes, pale (faded) complexion, short powdered wig, serious expression. Rather muddy colouring, not much modelling remaining, fuzzy eye outlines. Plain greenish-blue background.

Ivory: oval, 49 x 37mm ($1^{7}/_{8}$ x $1^{1}/_{2}$in), sight size, in a plain pinchbeck locket.

Prov: presumably by descent.

For the sitter, *see* SMM 18.

The traditional attribution is to Charles Shirreff, which may indeed be correct, but this miniature is a copy of the head-and-shoulders of a half-length portrait by John Opie at St Michael's Mount, which is itself a copy of a portrait by Sir Joshua Reynolds that Sir John gave to his cousin and friend, Sir Francis Basset, Lord de Dunstanville, but which has not been recorded since 1899. Since Reynolds's original was painted in 1786, and Opie's copy probably only a few years later, this miniature – if by Shirreff (a deaf-mute, like Richard Crosse) – would probably have been executed before his sojourn in India (1797–1809), very possibly after his move to Bath in 1794. A copy of this miniature, previously unidentified, is at Pencarrow.

I-1

SMM 22

Juliana Vinicombe, later Lady St Aubyn

Henry Bone, 1798

TQL to left in a white dress with blue sash and lace trimming, wearing a gold necklace and long white veil, seated on a red sofa with a black shawl over its arm. Blue eyes, fresh complexion, dark hair. Landscape through window to left, red curtain and stone column in right background.

Enamel: rectangle, 155 x 122mm ($6^{1}/_{8}$ x $4^{7}/_{8}$in), sight size; signed lower left: *HBone / 1798*, and inscr. on back: *Lady St. Aubyn / Enamel / Henry Bone / Hanover House / Hanover Square*.

Prov: probably commissioned by Sir John St Aubyn, 5th Baronet. Hung separately on the Staircase at St Michael's Mount.

Exh: Truro 1951 (7).

For the sitter, *see* SMM 19.

A copy of the portrait by Sir William Beechey at St Michael's Mount. Beechey exh. a *'Portrait of a Lady'* at the RA 1789, and a *'Portrait of a Young Lady'*, RA 1791, one probably the picture at St Michael's Mount. Henry Bone's preliminary drawing, squared and numbered for transfer to the enamel, and inscr.: *'Miss Vinicombe after Beechey for Sr J. St. Aubyn 1790 [erased] 1799'*, is in the NPG library (Bone Drawings I.89b).

Juliana's portrait, painted by Opie in 1797, in a white dress with red sash, is at St Michael's Mount (colour repr. in St Aubyn 1978, p.25). As a fellow-Cornishman, he gives her

much more character than in her somewhat simpering portrayal by Beechey, as reproduced by Bone. An oval half-length watercolour drawing of her as a young woman, by Henry Edridge, is in the National Gallery of Ireland, Dublin (*see* Le Harivel 1983, p.125, inv.269b). A later drawing of her by Edridge, whole-length seated with Sir John and their eldest son William, is repr. in Hartley 1977, p.80. A miniature head of her is listed in Wood 1789–1809, undated but probably *c.*1807–8.

SMM 23

Lady in a White Dress

Attributed to George Chinnery, *c.*1800

HS to right in a white frilly dress and light gold chain necklace. Dark greenish-brown eyes, pale complexion, black hair tied with yellow ribbon. Sky background.

Ivory: oval, 65 x 55mm (2⅝ x 2⅛in), sight size. Gold case.

Prov: uncertain.

Chinnery's work in miniature has not been systematically studied, but the traditional attribution here is probably correct, though an alternative suggestion might be John Comerford. The sitter appears to be a well-dressed young lady depicted *c.*1800, two years before Chinnery left Dublin (where he had gone in 1795) for London and then India. Comerford was working in Dublin at this time, and was greatly influenced by Chinnery. The miniature may, however, have been done during Chinnery's brief sojourn in London, between returning from Dublin in early 1802 and sailing to India in June, as there is no-one connected with the St Aubyns who is known to have been in Dublin at this period. Indeed, in terms of dress and style, this miniature compares very well with the more ambitious three-quarter-length that he did of Mrs Robert Sherson (Victoria & Albert Museum; *see* Archer 1979, p.359, pl.263) soon after arriving in Madras on 21 December 1802. More comparable in format, though the sitter is – unusually for a miniature – presented *en face*, is another miniature signed and dated by Chinnery as done in Madras in 1803, of *An Unknown Lady* (Christie's, 3 October 1972; Archer 1979, p.397, pl.309).

II-8

SMM 24

Miss St Aubyn

Henry Bone, 1809

See also colour plate 6.

TQL seated to left at a piano and holding a music score; she wears a low-cut white dress with blue sash. Pale grey eyes, pink complexion, luxuriant powdered hair dressed with pearls and high on top, a tress over her right shoulder. Red armchair to right, brownish-grey walls of the room behind.

Enamel: oval, 88 x 74mm (3½ x 2⅞in), signed at right above chair back: *HBone*, and inscr. on turquoise counter-enamel: *London / March 1809 / Painted by Henry Bone RA / Enamel painter to H.R.H. the Prince of Wales, after a / Miniature by S. Shelley*. Plain brass case.

Prov: commissioned by Sir John St Aubyn, 5th Bt., in 1809.

Henry Bone's preliminary drawing, in ink on transparent tracing paper, inscr. *'Miss St Aubyn for Sir John St (Aubyn after) Shelley – 1809 May 1'*, is in the NPG library (Bone Drawings III.12f). The whereabouts of Shelley's original miniature of *c.*1790 is not known (it is not at Pencarrow).

It seems likeliest that this is the eldest of the four daughters of Sir John St Aubyn, 4th Baronet, and his wife Elizabeth Wingfield: Elizabeth (b.1757, m. in 1790, Humphrey Prideaux), who is the one who would have been known simply as 'Miss St Aubyn', with no Christian name, prior to her marriage (and Bone was doubtless copying an inscription on the case of Shelley's original miniature when calling her so). But it might also be the second daughter, Catherine (d.1836), who gained some celebrity by her other artistic pursuits, painting and etching, and of whom her brother, the 5th Baronet – who was a keen collector of prints – might particularly have wanted to have a likeness. It was also she who, as co-heir of the 4th Baronet, and by her marriage in 1790 to her cousin, the Rev. John Molesworth, brought the St Aubyn estates into his family, thenceforward called the Molesworth-St Aubyns, with their chief seat at Pencarrow.

There is a *Self-Portrait* in oils by Catherine St Aubyn (the pendant to that of her husband) at Pencarrow, which agrees reasonably well with this miniature as a likeness of her.

I-3

SMM 25

Miss St Aubyn (Catherine, Mrs John Molesworth?)

British School, 19th century, after an original of *c.* 1790 (?)

HS to left in a pale yellow dress and white fichu. Grey eyes, pink complexion, luxuriant brown hair dressed with pearls. Golden background with opaque film over dark hatching on right.

Ivory: oval, 43 x 36mm (1 3/4 x 1 3/8in), sight size. Pinchbeck locket with green silk backing.

Prov: uncertain; perhaps originally the pendant of SMM 13?

Through some confusion, this miniature has been impossibly identified as being – like SMM 8 – of Barbara, Lady Molesworth. The sitter, however, appears to be the same as in SMM 24, shown from a different angle, but at about the same date, and with hair similarly dressed.

If so, it may have been a mix-up between Molesworths that accounted for the misidentification, suggesting that the 'Miss St Aubyn' of SMM 24 is indeed Catherine, rather than her elder sister Elizabeth. Catherine may in turn have been confused with her aunt and mother-in-law, Barbara, daughter of Sir John St Aubyn, 3rd Bt., who married Sir William Molesworth, 6th Bt., in 1762.

The handling of the miniature seems too loose for one of *c.*1790; it is not clear whether this is because it is a later copy of a lost original, or because it is a pastiche.

II–9

TRERICE

CORNWALL

Trerice – the typical Celtic prefix 'Tre' stands for 'homestead' or 'hamlet' – was a seat of one branch of the Cornish Arundells (not to be confused with another, that of the Arundells of neighbouring Lanherne, later of Wardour), from the reign of Edward III (1312–77) until 1768. The existing house was built by Sir John (IV) Arundell, and completed in 1573. It owes its preservation to the fact that when the family died out with John (VIII), 4th Baron Arundell, his heir, his wife's nephew William Wentworth, of Henbury in Dorset, let it to tenants. In 1802 it devolved upon Sir Thomas Dyke Acland, 10th Bt., of Killerton (*see* KIL 3), who used it as his headquarters for political forays into Cornwall. The Aclands sold the estate in 1915. The manor farm was bought by Cornwall County Council, which divided it into a number of smaller farms and sold off the house. After several changes of hand, it was purchased by the National Trust in 1953 from Somerset de Chair, with funds from the will of Mrs Annie Woodward; and in 1954 the new tenant, J.F. Elton, paid for the reinstatement of the two scrolled gables on the north front, which had been taken down after a gale in 1860.

The interiors contain some superb seventeenth-century plasterwork, but – unsurprisingly, after such a history – no indigenous contents. Gifts, bequests, and loans have made up the deficit.

Above left: the Hall
Above right: the east front

TRE 1
John Willey
Attributed to Edward Miles *c.*1790

HS to right in a brown coat and waistcoat, and white neckcloth. Pale grey eyes, white hair in queue, sallow face modelled with grey wash and short grey strokes, purple protruding lips, aged about 75. Grey scumbled background.

Ivory: oval, 41 x 31mm (1 5/8 x 1 1/4in), inscr. on the backing paper in ink: *Mr John Willey Surgeon / 4 Drury Lane, London. M. Mary Rhodes 1750 / b. 17 Oct 1717 / ob. 16 Oct 1794. My great grandfather. FBD.* Gilt composition neo-Rococo frame, with trade label of Thomas Beatty, 18 Warwick Street, Royal Leamington.

Prov: bequeathed to the National Trust by Miss Dickinson in 1993.

The miniature is unattributed, but bears a close resemblance to the work of Edward Miles in the 1790s.

John Willey (1717–94), Master Apothecary of Drury Lane, was apprenticed to Mr Edward Angier, 3 February 1736, and made a Freeman of the Society of Apothecaries, 5 November 1751. He m. in 1750, Mary Rhodes.

TRE/P/28

TYNTESFIELD

NORTH SOMERSET

The acquisition of Tyntesfield by the National Trust was one of the more sensational episodes, not just in its history and in that of the Trust, but also in that of the National Heritage Memorial Fund, whose crucial donation of three years' accumulated reserves made it possible. Identified as the last major High Victorian house to have survived with its character and historic contents still substantially intact, but with nineteen beneficiaries of the will of the 2nd Lord Wraxall to be bought out, the exchange of contracts on 15 June 2002 took place on a Saturday, after final negotiations lasting twenty-six hours.

Tyntesfield might be regarded as the exemplification in the west of England of the northern saying: 'Where there's muck, there's brass'. The enormous fortune of its builder, William Gibbs (1790–1875), was derived from a timely speculation in guano – solidified bird droppings from the barren islands off Peru – which was the most potent agricultural fertiliser before the development of artificial nitrates ('guano from Bristol' even features in chapter xxiii of Anthony Trollope's novel, *Barchester Towers*). With this money Gibbs bought the Regency Tudor house, Tyntes Place, in 1843, which he successively got John Gregory Crace (1809–89) to redecorate and refurnish from 1854 onwards, and George Plucknett of William Cubitt & Co. substantially to rebuild, to High Gothic plans by John Norton of Bristol, between 1863 and 1865.

William Gibbs (*see* TYN 18, 20, 24 & 25), his wife, *née* (Matilda) Blanche Crawley-Boevey (1817–87) of Flaxley Abbey (*see* TYN 19 & 26), and their son and successor, Antony (1841–1907) (*see* TYN 17 & 18), were leading and philanthropic High Anglicans. William

Left: the east front
Below: the Library

built, restored, or contributed to, more than nineteen churches, including Keble College Chapel in Oxford, and his last addition to Tyntesfield was its chapel, a *tour de force* of the Gothic Revival, designed by Arthur Blomfield and executed between 1872 and 1877. Antony Gibbs made many changes to Tyntesfield, but his most distinctive contribution was the Gothic furniture designed by the Devon-born Warwickshire upholsterer, James Plucknett (*c.*1836–1905), including a billiard table supported on small grouped Gothic columns, but incorporating electric scoring buttons.

The miniatures at Tyntesfield seem surprisingly sober after all this. Largely of members of the Gibbs and Crawley-Boevey families, they are almost all in copper or brass lockets, rather than gold, and are mostly by modest artists. There is an interesting echo of the original locus of William Gibbs's mercantile activities in Spain, in the group of portraits of him and his immediate family by Antonio Tomasich y Haro (TYN 24-27). However, all this is contradicted by the remarkable group of three substantial-sized miniatures by Sir William Ross (TYN 18-19 & 23). Framed in sumptuous neo-Rococo ormolu frames, and each preserved from light and damp by glazed ebony boxes with little doors, their freshness, brightness and refulgence were a revelation when first discovered in the Drawing Room cupboard, and continue to dazzle the eye now.

TYN 1
Captain John Woodward
British School, *c.*1760

HS to right in uniform (scarlet with black and silver facings), dark blue eyes, short grey wig, aged about 30. Grey stippled background, darker to left.

Ivory: oval, 39 x 34mm ($1^1/_2$ x $1^1/_4$ in), inscr. in brown ink on backing paper: *J / Woodward / the 70th Regt / died in the / West Indies / Lady C.* Oval copper frame.

Prov: entered the family collection through (Matilda) Blanche Crawley-Boevey, wife of William Gibbs.

Lit: Gibbs 1922, p.443, no.47 [a].

John Woodward (d.1764), of Ringwould in Kent, was the father of Mary Albinia (TYN 4), second wife of Sir Thomas Hyde Page of the Royal Engineers (a fine portrait of whom by James Northcote, formerly at Flaxley Abbey, was acquired for Tyntesfield by Richard, 2nd Baron Wraxall; *cf.* Miller 2003, pp.168-70, with colour pl.), whose daughter, also called Mary Albinia (TYN 15), became the wife of Sir Thomas Crawley-Boevey, 3rd Bt., and the mother of (Matilda) Blanche, wife of William Gibbs (TYN 19 & 26).

Captain Woodward was married to Catherine Monins. He died on active service on the island of Grenada. J.A. Gibbs (1922) listed a second miniature supposedly of this sitter, initialled and dated 1774 by Samuel Cotes, in the possession of Albinia Page and Marjorie Page (Mrs Stone), formerly of Clanna Cottage, Sydney, Gloucestershire.

TYN/53

TYN 2
Ann Savage, Lady Crawley-Boevey
Hannah Wollaston, *c.*1760

HS to left in a blue dress trimmed with white lace and pearls, single strand pearl necklace tied with blue ribbon and ear-drops, light brown eyes, dark brown hair dressed with a jewelled plume, aged about 20 to 25. Brown stippled background.

Ivory: oval, 41 x 34mm ($1^5/_8$ x $1^3/_8$ in), inscr. in brown ink on the vellum backing: *Hannah Woolaston*; and in a later hand: *Lady Crawley*. Plain oval copper frame, to match that of TYN 1.

Prov: entered the family collection through (Matilda) Blanche Crawley-Boevey, wife of William Gibbs.

Hannah Woolaston – or more probably Wollaston (the pronunciation as 'Woolaston' accounting for the misspelling) – is not otherwise recorded as a miniature painter; but it seems probable that she was a daughter of the portrait painter recorded by George Vertue, John Wollaston, Sr. (*c.*1672–after 1742). His son, also called John, whose existence Vertue does not mention, led an almost equally shadowy life before he left England in about 1749. Faber's engraving of his portrait of George Whitefield in the NPG is lettered: *John Wollaston Jnr. Pinxt. 1742*. He had a considerable practice (and influence on portrait painting) in the eastern United States, but returned to England in 1767, where the last sighting of him was in 1775. To judge from this one example, Hannah's approach to portraiture was as conventional as that of her putative brother. There is no known connection between the two John Wollastons and the William Wollaston (1693–1764), of Finborough Hall, Suffolk, of whom and whose wider family Hogarth painted a conversation piece in 1730.

Ann Savage (1745–1816) was the second, but only surviving, daughter and co-heiress of the Rev. Thomas Savage (1699/1700–60), Rector of Standish and Broadway, Gloucestershire, and Eleanor Barrow, daughter and heiress of Thomas Barrow, of Field Court, Gloucestershire. She m. in 1769, Thomas Crawley-Boevey (1743–1818), of Flaxley Abbey. Her first cousin once removed, Charles Barrow, the MP for the city of Gloucester in six successive Parliaments from 1751 to 1789, was created a baronet in 1784 with, in the absence of male issue, a special remainder to Ann's husband Thomas, who thus succeeded him as 2nd Bt. in 1789. She bore him thirteen children. Their eldest son, also called Thomas, the 3rd Bt. (1769–1847), was the father of (Matilda) Blanche Crawley-Boevey, wife of William Gibbs (TYN 19 & 26).

J.A. Gibbs (1922, p.440, no.11) lists no miniature of this sitter at Tyntesfield, but only an unattributed one in the possession of Cyril Pode, of Slade, Ivybridge, which (in his *Addenda & Corrigenda* of 1927, p.xvi) he ascribes to Northcote.

TYN/52

TYN 3

Man in Green

Attributed to Ozias Humphry, *c.*1770

See also colour plate 6.

HS to right, in a light green coat, white waistcoat and stock. Pale brown eyes, short powdered hair or wig, aged about 25. Light brown scumbled background, darker to left. Rather faded.

Ivory: oval, 39 x 31mm ($1\frac{1}{2}$ x $1\frac{1}{4}$ in). Oval gold frame, formerly part of a bracelet.

Prov: uncertain.

The colours of this miniature are slightly faded, but it is of high quality and, though unsigned with his usual monogram, is characteristic of Humphry's meticulous work of *c.*1770. The sitter's identity is unknown at present.

TYN/54

TYN 4

Mary Albinia Woodward, Lady Page

Manner of Nathaniel Hone, *c.*1780

HS to right, her left hand to cheek, in a pink dress with a black mourning ribbon on her right arm, and double strand pearl bracelet. Blue eyes, rosy complexion, and dark brown hair dressed with pearls and pink head-dress, aged about 20. Sky and trees background.

Ivory: oval (warped), 76 x 60mm (3 x $2\frac{3}{5}$ in). Oval gold frame with an elaborate back containing a plume of light brown hair, and also containing the monograms: *MAP* and *JM*, set in seed pearls, all mounted under white translucent glass within a dark blue glass oval.

Prov: entered the family collection through (Matilda) Blanche Crawley-Boevey, wife of William Gibbs.

Lit: Gibbs 1922, p.443, no.42 [b].

This miniature is skilfully painted and is very much in the style of Nathaniel Hone, but it is not really of high enough quality to justify a firm attribution.

Mary Albinia (1760–94) was the daughter of Captain John Woodward (TYN 1) and granddaughter of the Rev. R. Monins, of Ringwould and Charlton in Kent, 'heir male of the ancient family of Monins, of Waldershare Park' (later the seat of the Earls of Guilford). She m. in 1783, as his second wife, the military hero, engineer, author, and specialist in matters of drainage and wells, Thomas Hyde Page, who was knighted in the same year. The only one of his three wives to bear him children, she had eight, of whom three sons and two daughters survived infancy. One of these daughters, also called Mary Albinia, became the wife of Sir Thomas Crawley-Boevey, 3rd Bt., and the mother of (Matilda) Blanche, wife of William Gibbs. Thomas Hyde Page's first wife (whom he had married in 1777) was Susanna, the elder of the two sisters of Sir Thomas Crawley-Boevey, 2nd Bt., and widow of Edmund Bastard, of Kitley in Devon. Page was painted by Loutherbourg and Northcote; the latter portrait (inaccurately attributed to Reynolds in the old *DNB*) was acquired from Flaxley Abbey for Tyntesfield by Richard, 2nd Baron Wraxall. Mary Albinia was reputedly painted by Lawrence, but the half-length portrait of her in an oval, which shows her wearing a miniature of her husband at her breast, despite being inscribed as such, has nothing to do with that painter. She died at Tros-yr-afon House, Beaumaris, and was buried in the chancel of Beaumaris Church, where there is a memorial to her.

J.A. Gibbs (1922, p.443, no.42) lists three other anonymous miniatures of this sitter, two belonging to Henry Martin Gibbs, of Barrow Court in Somerset, and one in the possession of Albinia Page and Marjorie Page (Mrs Stone), formerly of Clanna Cottage, Sydney, Gloucestershire.

TYN/58

TYN 5

Elizabeth Farren, later Countess of Derby

After Sir Thomas Lawrence (1790)

HL standing to left, in a white fur-trimmed cloak, dark brown eyes, curly auburn hair, aged about 30. Discoloured sky background.

Ivory: oval, 103 x 82mm ($4\frac{1}{8}$ x $3\frac{1}{4}$ in), inscr. lower right with false signature: *R. Cosway*. Oval chased brass frame.

Prov: unknown, but on the vellum backing there are what appear to be a dealer's inscriptions in ink: *1148* and *US1/L*.

A debased version of Lawrence's famous 1790 whole-length portrait of *Elizabeth Farren* (Metropolitan Museum, New York, *cf.* Garlick 1989, no.294 & col.pl.5). The colouring in this miniature version has been drastically altered from Lawrence's original; the hair has become an untidy auburn mess, in place of Miss Farren's elegant windswept grey-powdered coiffure; and the attribution to Cosway can safely be discounted.

Elizabeth Farren (?1759–1829), Irish actress, first appeared in Bath in 1773, then in London in 1777, in *She Stoops to Conquer* at the Haymarket Theatre. She m. in 1797, as his second wife, Edward, 12th Earl of Derby, thus giving up her career on the stage. Neither she nor the Earls of Derby had any connection with the Gibbs family.

TYN/45

TYN 6

Army Officer

British School, *c.*1800–10

HS to left, but facing out, in scarlet uniform with blue facings, gold epaulettes, and white sword-belt with the regimental badge of an eleven-pointed white star with red, blue and gold centre. Blue eyes, grey hair in queue, dark heavy eyebrows, brownish complexion, aged about 30 to 40. Grey stippled background.

Ivory: oval, 74 x 62mm (2 x $2\frac{1}{2}$ in), sight size. Plain oval copper frame.

Prov: uncertain.

The sitter's identity is unknown at present, but because of the general style and apparent date of the miniature, he appears to be a middle-aged officer, perhaps serving in the Peninsular wars. It has been suggested, without much conviction and on the basis of the uniform, that he is a major in the Coldstream Guards and, because of the arrangement of the buttons, probably before the regulations passed in 1774, after which that regiment wore their buttons in pairs. However, the star on the sword-belt was also used by other regiments. The Gibbs family of Tyntesfield were a markedly unmilitary family. Apart from Blanche Gibbs's forebears, Sir Thomas Hyde Page and Captain John Woodward (*see* TYN 1), their own military connections appear to have been Scots. William Gibbs's uncle, Lord Justice Sir Vicary Gibbs, m. Frances Cerjat Kenneth

Mackenzie, who had two brothers – Col. Thomas Frederick Humberston Mackenzie (1753–83) and Lieut.-Gen. Francis Humberston Mackenzie, 1st Baron Seaforth and Chief of Clan Mackenzie (1754–1815) – and a sister, Helen, who m. Lieut.-Gen. Alexander Mackenzie Fraser of Inverallochy and Castle Fraser, MP (1756–1809). Relations between Gibbses and Frasers were close, particularly between William Gibbs's sister, Harriet, who m. George Gibbs of Belmont (TYN 7 & 21), and General Fraser's daughter, Helen. The General died at Sir Vicary Gibbs's house at Hayes in Middlesex, of an illness contracted on the ill-fated Walcheren Expedition, after which both his daughters made it their permanent home (*cf.* Gibbs 1922, pp.32 & 178-79). It does not seem impossible that one of these military men should be the sitter in this miniature, and that it should have passed to the Gibbs family through these ties of blood and friendship.

TYN/46

TYN 7

George Gibbs

James Leakey, 1802

HS to left, looking out, in a black coat and white stock. Hazel eyes, rosy complexion, dark brown hair, aged 20 to 25. Discoloured sky background.

Thinned oil: oval, 75 x 59mm (3 x 2¼ in), sight size. Plain oval copper frame, with printed label stuck to back: *George Gibbs / 18 / James Leakey.*

Prov: by inheritance to Henry Hucks Gibbs, 1st Lord Aldenham (1819–1907), from one of whose descendants acquired after 1927 for Tyntesfield.

Lit: Gibbs 1922, p.435, no.20 [c], as a miniature in oils in the possession of Lord Aldenham.

Leakey customarily painted in thinned oil, as in this and his other two miniatures at Tyntesfield (TYN 8 & 9).

George Gibbs (1779–1863), son of the Bristol merchant also called George Gibbs (1753–1818), of Redland, and partner from 1802 in his West Indian business, of which he succeeded him as head in 1818. First cousin of William Gibbs of Tyntesfield. He m. (1) *c.*1800, Salvina, daughter and heir of Henry Hendy of the Barbadoes; and (2) in 1814, William's sister, Harriet. In 1818 he established a new partnership in Bristol with Richard Bright, a city merchant and a partner in Harford's Bank. This partnership, named Gibbs, Bright & Gibbs, Merchants & Bankers, was ultimately absorbed by Antony Gibbs & Sons in 1881. In 1828, following the death of George Penrose Seymour, he rented Belmont from Seymour's son, the Rev. George Turner Seymour, who had built the predecessor of Tyntesfield, Tyntes Place, for himself and his wife, further along the same escarpment. After George Gibbs's death, William Gibbs used to stay there with his widow (who was also his sister) when he needed to supervise the building of Tyntesfield. After her death without children in 1865, it became the subsidiary house on the Tyntesfield estate.

J.A. Gibbs (1922, p.435, no.20) lists no portrait of this sitter at Tyntesfield, but includes a miniature by Leakey then with the 2nd Lord Aldenham, which was presumably this one. Lord Aldenham also owned seven volumes of the sitter's diaries (Gibbs 1932, p.26), and a copy of a miniature of the sitter by Sir William Ross dated 1851 (Gibbs 1922, p.435, no.20 [d]).

See also TYN 21.

TYN/38

TYN 8

Salvina Hendy, Mrs George Gibbs

James Leakey, 1802

HS to right, in a high-waisted white dress. Hazel eyes, rosy complexion, brown hair with centre parting, aged about 20. Discoloured sky background.

Thinned oil: oval, 73 x 60mm (2 ⅞ x 2⅜ in), sight size. Plain oval copper frame, backed with white glass, with plaited brown hair in oval centre; modern paper label stuck to back inscr. in blue ink: *Salvina Gibbs / born Hendy / 20.*

Prov: by inheritance to Henry Hucks Gibbs, 1st Lord Aldenham (1819–1907), from one of whose descendants acquired after 1927 for Tyntesfield.

Lit: Gibbs 1922, p.435, no.21 [a], as a miniature in oils in the possession of Lord Aldenham.

Salvina (1780–1809), daughter of Henry Hendy of the Barbadoes. She m. in 1802, as his first wife, George Gibbs (1779–1863; *see* TYN 7 & 21), but died without bearing him any children.

TYN/39

TYN 9

Joanna Gibbs

James Leakey, 1802

HS slightly to left, head turned to right, in a high-waisted white dress. Dark brown eyes, pink complexion, black hair piled high on crown, aged about 20. Discoloured sky background.

Thinned oil: oval, 73 x 60mm (2⅞x 2⅜ in), sight size. Plain oval copper frame, with plaited hair in reverse, and printed label stuck to the back: *Joanna Gibbs / James Leakey / 19*; and printed blue label of the Manchester Art Gallery (the Gallery has no record of any loan of this miniature), inscr. in ink: *3352.*

Prov: by inheritance to Henry Hucks Gibbs, 1st Lord Aldenham (1819–1907), from one of whose descendants acquired after 1927 for Tyntesfield.

Lit: Gibbs 1922, p.435, no.22 [a], as a miniature in oils in the possession of Lord Aldenham.

Joanna Gibbs (1777–1823) was the eldest daughter of the Bristol merchant, George Gibbs of Redland (1753–1818) and Esther Joanna Farr (1748–87). She went to live with her spinster aunt, Sibella (1760–1841) – a miniature of whom by Leakey was also owned by Lord Aldenham – and, like her, died unmarried.

TYN/41

TYN 10

Werrington Park, Cornwall

J. Owen, *c.* 1810–20

View of the house in a romantic park setting with a lake, fallow deer in the foreground, church to left, distant hills, and a cloudy sky.

Liquid oils on ivory: rectangle, 84 x 109mm (3¼ x 4¼ in), inscr. on the backing paper in pencil: *Werrington / Park / £2.2. / J. Owen.* Unframed, formerly in a single frame with TYN 11-13.

Prov: unknown.

This and the following three miniatures evidently all depict seats of the Dukes of Northumberland, painted in the early years of the nineteenth century. There is no J. Owen of this period recorded by Foskett, Schidlof, or Blättel as a miniaturist, nor does Thieme-Becker record one as a painter. The faint possibility is the architect Jacob Owen (North Wales 1778 – Tipton, Staffs. 1870), who, though that was his profession, would have received training in draughtsmanship after joining the Royal Engineers' Department of the Ordnance in 1804, and who is cited in the Rev. Thomas Mardy Rees's *Welsh Painters, Engravers, Sculptors (1527–1911)*, Carnarvon, 1912, albeit without any allusion to work in any of those three capacities. The miniatures were presumably painted for a member of the Percy family, but if so, there is no very obvious way in which they would have passed to the Gibbs family.

Werrington Park was the seat of the Morice family (*cf.* SMM 7-9). The last of them, the politician Sir Humphry Morice, (1723–85), a valetudinarian who left everything to his mistress, but for the provision of £600 a year for the care of his dogs and horses, sold it – and most importantly, the electoral patronage that went with it – to Hugh, 1st Duke of Northumberland in 1775.

TYN/1280A

TYN 11

Syon Park, Middlesex

J. Owen, *c.* 1810–20

View of the house from across the river, three cows on the far bank, the drive leading from the entrance door to a grey iron bridge, trees on either side, and a blue sky.

Liquid oils on ivory: rectangle, 84 x 109mm (3¼ x 4¼ in), inscr. on the backing paper in pencil: *Syon House / £2.2. / J. Owen.* Unframed, formerly in a single frame with TYN 10, 12 & 13.

Prov: unknown.

Syon Park has been a seat of the Percy Earls, and later Percy (Smithson) Dukes of Northumberland since 1594.

TYN/1280B

TYN 12

Warkworth Castle, Northumberland

J. Owen, *c.* 1810–20

View of the castle from across a river with sailing dinghy, a fisherman on the far bank, trees on either side, and a cloudy blue sky.

Liquid oils on ivory: rectangle, 84 x 109mm (3¼ x 4¼ in), uninscribed. Unframed, formerly in a single frame with TYN 10, 11 & 13.

Prov: unknown.

Warkworth Castle was a seat of the Percy family, later Earls and Dukes of Northumberland, from 1332. Its great period of building came after the Scottish invasion of 1383/4, under the 1st (1341–1408) and possibly the 2nd (1392/3–1455) Earls, father and son respectively of Harry 'Hotspur'. Its most impressive and beautiful feature, within and without, is the keep, seen here on the left. The castle now belongs to English Heritage.

There is less similarity between this view of Warkworth Castle and that, just titled *Warkworth Castle*, forming plate 23 of Charlotte Florentina, Duchess of Northumberland's *Castles of Alnwick, & Warkworth, &c.*, than there is between her and Owen's views of *Alnwick Castle from the North* (*see* TYN 13). But that is because this particular view appears to have been lithographed without any intervention of the Duchess. The plate instead says: 'Drawn on Stone by J.D. Harding, exactly copied on a reduced Scale from an Old Picture'. The composition looks like that of an oil painting dating from the eighteenth century, and – unlike Owen's view – it shows the Castle in a state of good repair. (Harding also drew on stone a view of Alnwick that he likewise claims to have been 'exactly copied on a reduced Scale from an Old Picture' – plate 5 – but it looks entirely spurious.)

TYN/1280C

TYN 13

Alnwick Castle, Northumberland

J. Owen, *c.*1810–20

View of the castle across a river with a stone bridge, trees on either side, and a cloudy blue sky.

Liquid oils on ivory: rectangle, 84 x 109mm (3¹/₄ x 4¹/₄ in), uninscribed. Unframed, formerly in a single frame with TYN 10, 11 & 12.

Prov: unknown.

Alnwick Castle has been a seat of the Percy family, later Earls and Dukes of Northumberland, since 1309. The view is across the River Aln from the north, and is interesting in that it shows the castle between the celebrated view painted from the same angle by Canaletto in 1751/2, and the heavy interventions by Anthony Salvin from 1854 onwards. It indicates the amount of work that was undertaken on the exterior for the 1st Duke (1715–86), from shortly after his inheritance in 1750 until his death, successively employing Daniel Garrett, James Paine, and Robert Adam, and the more local John Bell and Vincent Shepherd as executants. Most of their work, along with Robert Adam's extensive embellishments of the interiors in the late 1760s and early 1770s, were all swept away by Salvin for the 4th Duke, making this a rare record of what has gone.

There are interesting similarities between this view of Alnwick Castle and one painted (probably in watercolour) by Lady Charlotte Florentina Clive, Duchess of Northumberland (1787–1866), that was lithographed by J.D. Harding and printed by C. Hullmandel, as *Alnwick Castle, from the North Demesne*, as plate 2 of *Castles of Alnwick, & Warkworth, &c., from Sketches by C.F. Duchess of Northumberland. 1823*, privately printed by W. Nicol's Shakespeare Press in 1824 (there is no copy of this in the British Library, but there is one with a dedication, in part by hand, to her mother Henrietta Antonia, Countess of Powis, in the London Library). The link with Wales represented by the Duchess is an interesting one: might she have had, as a drawing-master, the otherwise unknown J. Owen, who painted these views of her husband's seats?

TYN/1280D

TYN 14

Madonna and Child with St John and a Goldfinch

After Raphael, early 19th century

WL figures of seated Madonna (in red dress with black and white collar, blue cloak, and white head-dress; brown eyes, auburn hair in plaits; holding a book in her left hand); infant St John the Baptist (in an animal skin; curly auburn hair; holding the goldfinch); and infant Christ; landscape with flowers, trees and a river, with a bridge to left, and buildings and mountains to right; cloudy blue sky.

Ivory: rectangle (slightly warped), 189 x 131mm (7³/₄ x 5¹/₂ in). Unframed.

Prov: unknown.

A nineteenth-century copy of Raphael's painting in the Uffizi, Florence. This famous work of art, painted around 1507 in Florence for Lorenzo Nasi, was a great favourite with foreign visitors to Italy, and was frequently copied. Bianca Boni was a copious generator of copies for the tourist trade in the first half of the nineteenth century, and this may possibly be one of her works, though she had many rivals.

TYN/1037

TYN 15

Mary Albinia Page, Lady Crawley-Boevey

H.J. Harding, *c.*1825

HS facing, head turned to left, gazing upwards with a soulful expression, in a black dress, white lace corsage and shawl, and white necklace, brooch and earring; light brown eyes, dark brown hair with elaborate coiffure and plaited hair bandeau, aged about 40. Red velvet curtain behind to left, base of column and sunset sky to right.

Ivory: oval, 95 x 77mm (3¹/₄ x 3 in), sight size, inscr. on the backing paper: *Mary Albinia / Crawley Boevey / daughter of Sir Thomas / Hyde Page and wife / of Sir Thomas Crawley Boevey Bt.* Oval copper frame.

Prov: entered the family collection through (Matilda) Blanche Crawley-Boevey, wife of William Gibbs.

Lit: Gibbs 1922, p.441, no.15 [e].

Mary Albinia (1784–1835) was one of the two daughters of Sir Thomas Hyde Page (1746–1821) by his second wife, Mary Albinia Woodward (d.1794, *see* TYN 4). She m. in 1807, Sir Thomas Crawley-Boevey, 3rd Bt. (1769– 1847), to whom she bore four sons and three daughters, the youngest of whom, (Matilda) Blanche (TYN 19 & 26), became the wife of William Gibbs.

J.A. Gibbs (1922, p.441, no.15) lists no less than four miniatures of Lady Crawley-Boevey in the possession of various people, all four of them by Harding. Arthur Crawley-Boevey (1898, p.317, no.317) mentions one by Sir William Ross, belonging to Henry Martin Gibbs of Barrow Court.

TYN/57

TYN 16

John Ley Gibbs

British School, *c.*1835

HS facing, in a blue coat with a black collar, green patterned waistcoat, white shirt with high collar, and black neck-cloth. Light blue eyes, dark brown hair and side-whiskers, aged about 40. Plain grey background.

Ivory: oval, 59 x 50mm (2¼ x 2 in), inscr. on the modern wooden backing: *John Ley Gibbs / b.1793 d.1837 / 93.* Plain oval brass frame.

Prov: by inheritance to Henry Hucks Gibbs, 1st Lord Aldenham (1819–1907), from one of whose descendants acquired after 1927 for Tyntesfield.

Lit: Gibbs 1922, p.436, no.32.

John Ley Gibbs (1793–1837) was the second son of the merchant navy officer, Captain William Gibbs (1757–1830), of Topsham in Devon, and Susanna Ley. He was thus a second cousin of William Gibbs of Tyntesfield, with whom he shared lodgings in Bloomsbury from 1812 to 1814. From then until 1834/5 he was in Genoa, originally as an employee, but from 1825 as a partner, of his uncle Lyle Gibbs. He m. in 1828, Ellen Maria, daughter of John Richard Gamble, of Finsbury Square, who bore him two surviving children, Ellin (1835–64) who died unmarried, and John Douglas Lyle (1833–91) who married, but had no children. With his death the Topsham line of the Gibbs family became extinct, after six generations. J.A. Gibbs (1922, Appendix III, p.436, no.32) recorded an anonymous miniature of this sitter in the possession of Lord Aldenham, but no other in the possession of George Abraham Gibbs at Tyntesfield or with any other member of the family. As with other such cases amongst the miniatures catalogued here (*see* TYN 7-9), one can only conclude that one of the Lords Aldenham transferred them to Lord Wraxall some time after 1927 (the date of J.A. Gibbs's *Addenda & Corrigenda*).

TYN/51

TYN 17

Antony Gibbs

British School, 1844

HS facing, as a child in a white dress. Hazel eyes, cloud of golden curls, aged 3. Sky background.

Ivory: oval, 43 x 37mm (1¾ x 1½ in), sight size. Plain oval copper frame, with a lock of hair in the back, and a typed inscription: *Antony Gibbs / 1844.*

Prov: probably commissioned by his parents, and thence by descent.

The artist of this idealised 'goldilocks' portrait is unknown at present, though a search of the family archive may prove fruitful. An unlikely attribution to the Spanish miniaturist Antonio Tomasich y Haro has been suggested. J.A. Gibbs records a portrait in oils of Antony Gibbs as a child, by John Phillip, but no miniature other than that by Sir William Ross (*see* TYN 18; Gibbs 1932, p.65).

Antony (1841–1907), eldest son and heir of William Gibbs (1790–1875) and his wife, (Matilda) Blanche, *née* Crawley-Boevey (1817–87). He was no good at figures, so did not enter the family firm, but became a considerable Bristol figure, as a magistrate and an important contributor to local charitable and religious affairs. He was brought up at Tyntesfield, moved to nearby Charlton in 1869, and married Janet Louisa Merivale in 1872. Antony and his architect, Henry Woodyer, remodelled Charlton and made radical alterations to Tyntesfield, which he moved into after the death of his mother in 1887. He also commissioned a series of remarkable pieces of Gothic-style furniture for Charlton and Tyntesfield, designed by the Devon-born but Warwickshire-based James Plunkett, cabinet-maker and upholsterer; and added a succession of *objets d'art*, Old Master paintings, and both British and Continental watercolours to the collection. He also greatly extended the gardens and hothouses, and kept everything up in a manner that was 'not excelled in the West Country' (*Country Life*, 17 May 1902). Continuing his father's tradition of philanthropy with his brother Henry Martin, he paid for the Hall, Library, Common Rooms and Kitchen at Keble College, Oxford; and rebuilt Wraxall Church to the designs of Sir Arthur Blomfield in the 1890s.

TYN/50

TYN 18

William Gibbs with his two eldest children, Dorothea and Antony

Sir William Ross, 1849

See also colour plate 7.

Three WL figures, the two children either side of their father, sitting on a crimson sofa, landscape and sky background to the left, and a crimson curtain to right.

Ivory: circle, 255mm (10in) diameter, sight size, in a rectangular Rococo ormolu and silver frame, with a hinged black wooden case.

Prov: by descent.

Exh: Society of Arts 1860 (posthumous exhibition of Sir William Ross's works).

Lit: Gibbs 1922, p.435, no.14 [c]; 1932, p.65, no.1 & p.66. no.7. Miller 2003, p.57 & col.pl.p.55.

In complete contrast to the other, infinitely more modest, miniatures at Tyntesfield, are this and the other two miniatures by Sir William Ross (*see* TYN 19 & 23), two of them painted when the artist came to stay for six weeks in 1849, and the third three years later. Each encased in a sumptuous neo-Rococo ormolu frame, and protected by a glazed ebony box with little doors, their freshness and colours still have the same impact as the polychromy of marble and stained glass must once have had in the Chapel. Nonetheless, by their very nature, these boxed miniatures by the miniature painter to Queen Victoria, though rare and

precious, were not ostentatious but private, and celebrated the simple domestic pleasure of joy in affectionate children.

William (1790–1875), as the paterfamilias, is shown here with his eldest son and eventual successor, Antony (1841–1907), and with his eldest child, Dorothea Harriett (1840–1914). Sadly, a later photograph taken in the latter part of the 1860s (*see* Miller 2003, p.87) shows her to have grown up into a rather dumpy, slightly pug-nosed woman. It may have been this that accounted for the fact that she died unmarried.

Sir William Ross was almost house miniature-painter to the Gibbs family and their kin: J.A. Gibbs (1922) lists nearly thirty miniatures of them by him.

TYN/275

TYN 19

(Matilda) Blanche Gibbs with her children, Alice, George and William

Sir William Ross, 1849

See also colour plate 7.

Four nearly WL figures, the mother with two children either side of her, and one on her lap, sitting on a crimson sofa, landscape and sky background to the left, and gold curtain to the right.

Ivory: circle, 255 (10in) diameter, sight size, in a frame and case to match TYN 18.

Prov: by descent.

Exh: Society of Arts 1860 (posthumous exhibition of Sir William Ross's works).

Lit: Gibbs 1922, p.435, no.15 [e]; 1932, p.66, nos.3 & 4, and p.97, no.1. Miller 2003, p.57 and col.pl.p.55.

This miniature was painted in 1849 to match its companion, TYN 18. Alice Blanche (1843–71), the Gibbs's second daughter, leans on her mother, who holds her hand. The newest-born child, George Abraham (1848–70), sits on a cashmere shawl on his mother's lap. He is embraced by the second son, William (1846–69). Alice m. in 1866, the Rev. Alfred Gurney (1843–98), curate of the most advanced Tractarian church in London, St. Barnabas in Pimlico (from whose mother church, St. Paul's in Knightsbridge, Bishop Blomfield had earlier forced its builder, the Rev. William Bennett, to resign). George joined Antony Gibbs & Sons, but contracted yellow fever on his return from South America, and died in Kingston, Jamaica. William, who later had to leave Dublin University because of ill health, subsequently died at Tyntesfield.

TYN/276

TYN 20

William Gibbs

George Hughes, 1850

HS to left, in a black coat, grey waistcoat, black bow tie, and white shirt with ruffled front and high collar. Brown eyes, sparse grey hair brushed forward and side-whiskers, aged 60. Plain dark brown background.

Ivory: oval, 94 x 74mm ($3\frac{3}{4}$ x $2\frac{7}{8}$ in), sight size. Plain oval copper frame, with printed catalogue cutting: *WM. GIBBS / Painted by HUGHES 1850.*

Prov: by descent.

William Gibbs (1790–1875), second son of Antony (1756–1815), who was the founder of the trading company, Antony Gibbs & Sons (specialising in Iberian and South American business), and of Dorothea Barnetta Hucks (1760–1820). William himself set up trading companies in Cadiz and Gibraltar, before returning to the chief family firm in London in 1822. He and his elder brother, (George) Henry, took advantage of the break-up of the Spanish Empire to greatly expand the business on the Pacific coast of South America. In 1840 their agents in Lima locked them into long-term contracts for the export of guano (solidified bird-droppings) from barren islands off the coast of Peru to England, for use as fertiliser. Although these contracts could have been disastrous, they turned out to be so profitable that, between the landing of the first shipments in 1842 and 1875, the partners were clearing about £100,000 per annum.

William m. in 1839, (Matilda) Blanche Crawley-Boevey (1817–87), and in 1843 they acquired Tyntes Place, which, after its spectacular transformation into the Gothic Revival extravaganza of Tyntesfield between 1863 and 1865, remained the family home until its acquisition by the National Trust in 2002.

TYN/40

TYN 21

George Gibbs

British School, *c.* 1850

HS slightly to left, in a dark blue coat with black collar, dark grey waistcoat, black neck-cloth, and white shirt with high collar. Blue eyes, short wavy grey hair, aged about 70. Plain brown background.

Enamel: oval, 50 x 44mm (2 x 1½ in), uninscribed on the counter-enamel, but with a paper label inscr.: *£10.10*. Plain oval copper frame with cracked glass.

Prov: by inheritance and descent.

J.A. Gibbs records no enamel miniature of George Gibbs. However, as he says that, apart from copies belonging to Lord Aldenham which are marked by a symbol, 'no copies other than replicas by the original artists are mentioned' (1922, p.433), this could be a copy in enamel of the miniature of George Gibbs by Sir William Ross dated 1851, of which he notes only a copy in the collection of Lord Aldenham (1922, p.435, no.20 [d]).

For the sitter, *see* TYN 7.

TYN/44

TYN 22

Albinia Crawley-Boevey, Mrs George Daubeny

Magdalena (Ross) Dalton, after Sir William Ross, *c.* 1850

HS to left in a grey dress and lace collar, pinned with a brooch. Grey eyes, dark brown hair with centre parting and ringlets over ears, aged about 30.

Ivory: oval, 93 x 76mm (3⅝ x 3 in), sight size, with an identifying pencil inscription on the back repeating a printed catalogue cutting: *ALBINIA DAUBENY / Painted by Miss Dalton / from a miniature by Sir W.C. ROSS*. Plain oval copper frame.

Prov: by gift (?) and then by descent.

Lit: ? Gibbs 1922, p.442, no.31 [c], as an original miniature by Sir William Ross.

J.A. Gibbs (1922, p.442, no.31 [b]) referred to the original of this miniature as being in the possession of the Rev. George W. Daubeny, of Knodishall, Saxmundham. He also recorded another autograph miniature by Sir William Ross at Tyntesfield, but it was probably in fact this copy. Magdalena Ross, who m. in 1841/2, Edwin Dalton, was a sister of the famous Victorian miniaturist, Sir William Ross. In 1932, J.A. Gibbs recorded a number of other copies in miniature by 'Miss Ross' (whom he mistakenly assumed to have been Sir William's daughter), in the possession of Lord Cullen, the grandson of George Henry Gibbs (1785–1842) and Caroline Crawley (1794–1850).

Albinia Anne (1810–50) was the eldest daughter of Sir Thomas Crawley-Boevey, 3rd Bt. and Mary Albinia Page (*see* TYN 15), and the sister of (Matilda) Blanche, who married William Gibbs. She m. in 1843, the Rev. George Barnston Daubeny (1812–69), eldest son of the Rev. George William Daubeny (1784–1860), of Seend House in Wiltshire, and Elizabeth Crawley, and great-nephew (?) of the Rev. Charles Daubeny (1745–1827), Archdeacon of Salisbury and Vicar of North Bradley and of Road, Wiltshire, who married a Miss Barnston.

There was an aptness to this connection with Blanche Gibbs, as the church-building and tractarianism undertaken by her and her husband were prefigured by the activities and attitudes of Charles Daubeny, who – amongst other such acts – built the first free and open church in the country, Christ Church, Walcot, for the poor of Bath, and of whom the *DNB* says: 'In his theories of the dignity and importance of the church and her ministers, he anticipated the tractarian party'.

TYN/1056

TYN 23

George Abraham and Henry Martin Gibbs as children

Sir William Ross, 1852

See also colour plate 8.

Two WL figures with a large dog, under a tree in a park landscape; the elder boy holding the dog under its chin with one hand and its chain with the other; the younger boy seated on the ground, holding a plucked daisy aloft. Cloudy sky.

Ivory: circle, 255 (10in) diameter, sight size, in a frame and case to match TYN 18 & 19.

Exh: Society of Arts 1860 (posthumous exhibition of Sir William Ross's works), as *The Sons of W. Gibbs Esq.*

Lit: Gibbs 1932, p.66, no.4, and p.84, no.1. Miller 2003, p.57 and col.pl.p.55.

Painted three years after Ross's first visit to Tyntesfield in 1849, to match TYN 18 & 19.

George Abraham (1848–70), for the sitter, *see* TYN 19. Henry Martin (1850–1928) was close to his eldest brother Antony, with whom he visited Italy in 1874, acquiring Renaissance *objets de virtù* on their travels, and joining with him to pay for the Hall, Library, Common Rooms and Kitchen of Keble College, Oxford. He also paid for buildings at two Woodard foundations, Lancing and Ardingly Colleges, and restored the Garrison Church at Dover Castle. He subsequently set up his own establishment at Barrow Court in Somerset, and paid for the restoration of the church and other buildings in Barrow Gurney.

TYN/277

TYN 24

William Gibbs

Antonio Tomasich y Haro, 1872

HS to right, in a dark blue coat. Light brown eyes, grey hair, and bushy grey beard, aged 82. Plain grey background.

Ivory: oval, 66 x 52mm ($2\frac{5}{8}$ x 2 in), sight size, signed and dated lower right: *A. Tomasich 1872.* Plain oval brass frame engr.: *William Gibbs / of Tyntesfield / A. Tomasich / 34*.

Prov: possibly commissioned by Henry Martin Gibbs, and thence by inheritance and descent.

Lit: Gibbs 1922, p.435, no.14 [a] or [c]; Miller 2003, p.99 and col.pl.p.98.

Tomasich was evidently a slow worker, as William's diary entry for 14 June 1872 records: 'Gave Tomasich another, and I hope the last, sitting of $1\frac{1}{2}$ hours, and he gave me hopes that he would tell Henry on Monday that the miniatures were finished.' But four days later he wrote in exasperation: 'Tomasich came again and I gave him an 11th sitting of $1\frac{3}{4}$ hours, but it really is terribly tiresome work in this broiling heat, and I am heartily sick of it.'

These entries would seem to establish not only that this is the prime version of Tomasich's miniature of William Gibbs, and that TYN 25 is a repetition of it, but also that the sittings were at the behest of Henry, William's fourth son. J.A. Gibbs (1922) listed the version in the possession of Lord Aldenham as the prime one, that at Tyntesfield as a replica of it, and the one in the possession of Henry (Martin) Gibbs without comment. However, he gives no dates for any of them, and it is therefore impossible to tell which version was which, or how he arrived at his ranking.

For the sitter, *see* TYN 20; and for the artist, *see* TYN 25.

TYN/47

TYN 25

William Gibbs

Antonio Tomasich y Haro, *c.*1876 (?)

See also colour plate 6.

HS to right, in a dark blue coat. Light brown eyes, grey hair, and bushy grey beard, aged 82. Plain grey background.

Ivory: oval, 66 x 52mm ($2\frac{5}{8}$ x 2 in), sight size, signed and dated: *A. Tomasich, 1871* [?]. Plain oval copper frame.

Prov: by descent.

Lit: Gibbs 1922, p.435, no.14 [b].

Antonio Tomasich y Haro, whose name suggests a man whose father was from one of the Slavonic Habsburg lands and his mother from Spain, painted in that country and in the Hispanic territories of Mexico and Cuba. Despite the fact that he did practise elsewhere in England, it was probably through a Spanish connection that he came to the notice of William Gibbs. Although the present miniature appears to be dated 1871, it was in 1872 that he was first mentioned in William's diary. Given that it is identical to TYN 24, which bears that date, it may be a repetition of it, with the date (originally 1876?, like that of its pendant, TYN 26) damaged or distorted, to read as 1871.

For the sitter, *see* TYN 20.

TYN/55

TYN 26

(Matilda) Blanche Crawley-Boevey, Mrs William Gibbs

Antonio Tomasich y Haro, 1876

HS to left, in a dark blue dress with a large bejewelled cross, and a white and blue head-dress. Hazel eyes, smooth grey hair, aged 59. Light grey background.

Ivory: oval, 73 x 60mm ($2\frac{7}{8}$ x $2\frac{3}{8}$ in), sight size, signed and dated lower left: *A. Tomasich 1876.* Plain oval copper frame.

Prov: by descent.

Lit: Gibbs 1922, p.435, no.15 [g]; Miller 2003, p.99 and col.pl.p.98.

(Matilda) Blanche (1817–87), third and youngest daughter of Sir Thomas Crawley-Boevey, 3rd Bt. (1769–1847), of Flaxley Abbey in Gloucestershire, and Mary Albinia Page (*see* TYN 15). She m. in 1839, William Gibbs (1790–1875), then living at 16 Hyde Park Gardens in London, senior partner in the family business, and shortly to transform the Gibbs fortunes, enabling them to acquire Tyntes Place and rebuild it as Tyntesfield.

Blanche Crawley-Boevey came from the family of Boeveys or Boveys, who were long established at Flaxley Abbey. One of her forebears, Catharina or Katharine Riches (1669–1726/7), for seven years the wife of William Bovey, was celebrated for her good works during her thirty-five year widowhood, including buying an estate to augment the income of Flaxley Church. For her, and for genealogies of the Crawleys, Boeveys, and related families, *see* Crawley-Boevey 1898. She is commemorated on a monument by Gibbs and Rysbrack in Westminster Abbey, and on another at Flaxley, both put up at the expense of her lifelong friend, Miss Mary Pope. (The two ladies were, however, caricatured by Addison in *The Spectator*, as 'The Perverse Widow' – who resisted the blandishments of Sir Roger de Coverley – and her 'Malicious Confidante'). On her death, Thomas Crawley, a London merchant's son, inherited Flaxley, and added the name of Boevey to his own. His grandson, also called Thomas, succeeded by special remainder to the baronetcy conferred on his kinsman, Charles Barrow, MP.

Blanche supported William Gibbs in his charitable activities and church-building. The second church that they had transformed in true tractarian form, by (Sir) George Gilbert Scott, was Flaxley (1856), replacing the previous chapel designed by Katharine Bovey. In thanks for this, the Crawley-Boeveys gave Tyntesfield one of its greatest treasures. The Flaxley Casket, an apparently medieval metal casket decorated with ivory panels depicting *The Romance of the Knight of the Swan* (Wagner's 'Lohengrin'), assumed pride of place in the Drawing Room.

When William Gibbs died in 1875, he bequeathed Tyntesfield not to his eldest son Antony, but to Blanche, who resided there till her death in

1887. She continued her husband's tradition of architectural philanthropy, building almshouses, a village club, a cottage convalescent home, and a temperance inn (named the Battle Axes, after the chief charge on the Gibbs coat-of-arms) in Wraxall; and St. Michael's Home for Consumptives at Axbridge, as a memorial both to William and to the daughter whom they had lost to tuberculosis, Albinia (*see* TYN 27). She also commissioned, from John Henry Lorimer, the portrait of her kinswoman, friend, and fellow-disciple of John Keble, the prolific and popular novelist, Charlotte M. Yonge (1882), which is still at Tyntesfield.

It seems likely that this miniature is a replica of the one painted for the sitter's fourth son, Henry Martin Gibbs, in 1872 (*cf.* TYN 24) and recorded by J.A. Gibbs (1922, p.435, no.15 [f]), as William Gibbs's diary for that year records regular sittings by Blanche and her daughter Albinia between 17 June and 11 July. This repetition was probably executed for the sitter herself.

TYN/48

TYN 27

Albinia Anne Gibbs

Antonio Tomasich y Haro, 1876

HS to right, in a blue dress and white lace collar, with a large bejewelled cross on a gold chain round her neck. Hazel eyes, thick plaited brown hair, aged about 20. Grey background.

Ivory: oval, 73 x 59mm (2 7/8 x 2 3/8 in), signed and dated middle right: *A. Tomasich 1876*, and inscr. in brown ink on the separate parchment backing: *Miniature of the late Mr Albinia Page, Aged 16 years & afterwards the wife of Sr Jn G. Boevey who died Feby the 16th 1835.* Plain oval copper frame.

Prov: by inheritance.

Mary Albinia Page did indeed die on 16 February 1835, but she was the wife of Sir Thomas Crawley-Boevey, 3rd Bt., not Sir John, and this miniature is clearly not of her (for an authentic likeness, *see* TYN 15). It seems possible that the writer of the inscription, at sea as to the date of the miniature, and knowing it to be of an Albinia, identified it impossibly with Albinia Page, rather than, as should have been done, with Albinia Gibbs (1853–74).

For we know from William Gibbs's diary that Tomasich had regular sittings with Albinia and her mother Blanche between 17 June and 11 July 1872. As in the case of her mother's miniature (TYN 26), the original of 1872 is not at Tyntesfield, probably because they both seem to have been painted for William's fourth son Henry, rather than for either William himself or the sitters. Indeed, J.A. Gibbs (1932, p.66, no.10) only records a version by then in the possession of Henry's eldest son, Lt.-Col. William Otter Gibbs. The present miniature is probably a replica, painted for the sitter's mother after Albinia's death from tuberculosis in 1874. Blanche Gibbs also paid for the building of St. Michael's Home for Consumptives at Axbridge, as a memorial to her husband and her daughter.

TYN/49

TYN 28

The Hon. Doreen Albinia De Burgh Gibbs, later the Hon. Mrs Norman, as a child

M.P. or M.R., 1917

WL standing in a white fur coat and hat, holding an ermine muff. Brown eyes, shoulder-length golden hair, aged about 4 or 5. Unfinished background.

Ivory: rectangle, 148 x 109mm (5 5/3 x 4 1/4 in), signed mid-right: *M.P.* or *M.R.* Gilded copper frame in a hinged leather case.

Prov: by inheritance.

Lit: Gibbs 1932, p.68, no.32.

The Hon. Doreen Gibbs (b.1913) is the only daughter of the Right Hon. George Abraham Gibbs, 1st Baron Wraxall (of Somerset) (1873–1931), the eldest son of Antony Gibbs (*see* TYN 17) and Janet Merivale, and his first wife Victoria Florence de Burgh Long (1880–1920), eldest daughter of the Right Hon. Walter Long, later Viscount Long of Wraxall (in Wiltshire). She m. in 1937, the barrister Charles Bathurst Norman, younger son of the Rev. Harry Norman of Iwood Manor, Somerset, and has a son and a daughter.

Much cherished by her parents, and by her father alone after her mother's untimely death, she was the subject of five portraits recorded in his possession by J.A. Gibbs in 1932. Three were miniatures, including this one, but even then the name behind the initials M.P. – or M.R., as J.A. Gibbs read them – had been lost.

TYN/4182

Plate 1: *clockwise from top left* [actual size]

ALA 7 (p.10) **Rebecca Parminter** British School, *c.* 1750
ALA 8 (p.10) **Young Man in a Red Coat** Manner of Gervase Spencer, *c.* 1760
ANT 2 (p.13) **Lord Keeper Coventry** Attrib. to Laurence Hilliard, *c.* 1625
ANT 16 (p.17) **Letitia Trelawney** Bernard Lens, *c.* 1720–30
ANT 25 (p.19) **Hon. Caroline Pole-Carew** Elizabeth Paye, 1808

Plate 2: *clockwise from top left* [actual size]

ANT 9 (p.15) **Called 'Sir John Carew'** Samuel Cooper, *c.* 1660
ANT 10 (p.15) **Sarah, Lady Carew** Samuel Cooper, *c.* 1662
ANT 39 (p.22) **Lady Beatrice Butler** Annie Howard, 1889

Plate 3: [approx. 70% actual size]
ARL 7 (p.27) Amelia Onslow, Mrs Thomas Chamberlayne Sir William Ross, 1833

Plate 4: *left to right* [approx. 70% actual size]

KIL 4 (p.36) **Lydia (Hoare), Lady Acland** Attrib. to George Sanders, *c.*1808

KNI 1 (p.43) **Samuel Amory** Alfred Edward Chalon, 1826

Plate 5: *clockwise from top* [actual size]

CDO 6 (p.32) **Basil Drewe** Gordon Chase, 1906
COS 5 (p.40) **Unknown Young Man** British School, *c.*1830–35
SMM 4 (p.55) **Charles I** English School, 1648
SMM 15 (p.58) **Lady in Blue** Attrib. to Jeremiah Meyer, *c.*1775
SMM 1 (p.54) **Lady Anne Clifford** Attrib. to Peter Oliver, 1620

Plate 6: *clockwise from top left* [actual size]

SMM 24 (p.60) **Miss St Aubyn** Henry Bone, 1809
LAN 8 (p.46) **Hon. Charles Bagenal Agar** British School, *c.*1810
TYN 25 (p.72) **William Gibbs** Antonio Tomasich y Haro, *c.*1876
TYN 3 (p.65) **Man in Green** Attrib. to Ozias Humphry, *c.*1770

Plate 7: *left to right* [approx. 25% actual size]
TYN 18 (p.69) William Gibbs with his two children, Dorothea and Antony Sir William Ross, 1849
TYN 19 (p.70) (Matilda) Blanche Gibbs with her children, Alice, George and William Sir William Ross, 1849

Plate 8: [approx. 50% actual size]
TYN 23 (p.71) George Abraham and Henry Martin Gibbs Sir William Ross, 1852

BIBLIOGRAPHY

Acland 1981 Anne Acland, *A Devon Family: The Story of the Aclands*, Chichester, 1981.

***A la Ronde* 1993** Hugh Meller, *A la Ronde*, NT guidebook, 1993.

***Antony* 1992** Oliver Garnett and Alastair Laing, *Antony*, NT guidebook, 1992.

Archer 1979 Mildred Archer, *India and British Portraiture 1770–1825*, London, 1979.

***Arlington Court* 1999** Alastair Laing, Hugh Meller, Steve Mulberry and Simon Stevens, *Arlington Court*, NT guidebook, 1999.

Auerbach 1961 Erna Auerbach, *Nicholas Hilliard*, London, 1961.

Auerbach and Adams 1971 Erna Auerbach and C. Kingsley Adams, *Paintings & Sculpture at Hatfield House*, London, 1971.

Binney 2002 Marcus Binney (ed.), *The Tyntesfield Emergency*, London, 2002.

Blättel 1992 Harry Blättel, *International Dictionary: miniature painters, silhouettists*, Munich, 1992.

Bourdeau 1895 J. Bourdeau, *La Rochefoucauld*, Paris, 1895.

Caffrey 2000 Paul Caffrey, *Treasures to Hold: Irish and English Miniatures 1650–1850 from the National Gallery of Ireland Collection*, Dublin, 2000.

***Castle Drogo* 1995** Hugh Meller, *Castle Drogo*, NT guidebook, 1995.

***Charles I* 1972** Oliver Millar, *The Age of Charles I: Painting in England 1620–1649*, exh. cat., Tate Gallery, 1972.

Chichester 1871 Sir Alexander Bruce Chichester, *History of the Family of Chichester from AD 1086 to 1870*, London, 1871.

***Clifford* 1990** Abbot Hall Art Gallery, *"Proud Northern Lady": Lady Anne Clifford 1590–1676*, exh. cat., Kendal, 1990.

Corp 2001 Edward Corp, *The King over the Water: Portraits of the Stuarts in Exile after 1689*, Edinburgh, 2001.

Crawley-Boevey 1898 Arthur W. Crawley-Boevey, *The 'Perverse Widow': being Passages from the Life of Catharina, Wife of William Boevey, Esq., of Flaxley Abbey, in the County of Gloucester, with Genealogical Notes on that Family and others connected therewith*, London, New York & Bombay, 1898.

Diderot 1979 Denis Diderot, *Salons. Diderot: Vol.2.* 1765, Oxford, 1979.

***Dobson* 1983–4** Malcolm Rogers, *William Dobson 1611–46*, exh. cat., NPG, London, 1983.

Edmond 1983 Mary Edmond, *Hilliard and Oliver: the lives and works of two great miniaturists*, London, 1983.

Farington 1978–84 Kathryn Cave, Kenneth Garlick and Angus Macintyre (eds.), *The Diary of Joseph Farington*, New Haven, 1978–84.

Fenlon 2001 Jane Fenlon, *The Ormonde Picture Collection*, Kilkenny, 2001.

Foskett 1964 Daphne Foskett, *John Smart: The man and his miniatures*, London 1964.

Foskett 1974 Daphne Foskett, *Samuel Cooper and his contemporaries*, London, 1974.

Foskett 1987 Daphne Foskett, *Miniatures: Dictionary and Guide*, Woodbridge, 1987.

Garlick 1989 Kenneth Garlick, *Sir Thomas Lawrence: a complete catalogue of the oil paintings*, Oxford, 1989.

Gibbs 1922 John Arthur Gibbs, *The History of Antony and Dorothea Gibbs and of their contemporary relatives, including the history of the origin & early years of the House of Antony Gibbs and Sons*, London, 1922.

Gibbs 1932 John Arthur Gibbs, *Pedigree of the Family of Gibbs of Pytte* *in the parish of Clyst St George. Compiled by Lord Aldenham, F.S.A.*, 3rd edn., London, 1932.

Gilbert and Gourdault 1883 D.L. Gilbert and J. Gourdault, *Oeuvres de la Rochefoucauld*, Paris, 1883.

Gluck 1931 Gustav Gluck, *Van Dyck: des Meisters Gemälde (Klassiker der Kunst)*, Stuttgart, 1931.

Gower 1891 Lord Ronald Gower (ed.), *Stafford House Letters*, London, 1891.

Hartley 1977 Diana Hartley, *The St Aubyns of Cornwall 1200–1977*, Chesham, 1977.

***Jones Collection* 1923** Anon., *Jones Collection, Part III*, Victoria & Albert Museum, London, 1923

Kerslake 1977 John Kerslake, *Early Georgian Portraits*, London, 1977.

***Killerton* 2000** Anon., *Killerton House*, NT guidebook, 2000.

***Knightshayes Court* 1999** Hugh Meller and Alastair Laing, *Knightshayes Court*, NT guidebook, 1999.

***Lanhydrock* 1995** Michael Trinick *et al.*, *Lanhydrock*, NT guidebook, 1995.

Lees-Milne 1985 James Lees-Milne, *Midway on the Waves*, London, 1985.

Le Harivel 1983 Adrian Le Harivel, *Illustrated Summary Catalogue of Drawings, Watercolours and Miniatures*, National Gallery of Ireland, Dublin, 1983.

Long 1929 Basil Long, 'Richard Crosse, miniaturist and portrait-painter', *Walpole Society Journal*, London, 1929, vol.XVII, pp.61-94.

Long 1930 Basil S. Long, *Hand-List of Miniature Portraits and Silhouettes*, London, 1930.

***Lytes Cary* 1977** Dudley Dodd, *Lytes Cary*, NT guidebook, 1977.

Mathew 1981 W.M. Mathew, *The House of Gibbs and the Peruvian Guano Monopoly*, London, 1981.

***Mauritshuis* 1977** Anon., *Mauritshuis: The Royal Cabinet of Paintings illustrated general catalogue*, The Hague, 1977.

McAleer 1958 Edward C. McAleer, *The Sensitive Plant: A Life of Lady Mount Cashell*, Chapel Hill, 1958.

Millar 1995 Delia Millar, *The Victorian Watercolours and Drawings in the Collection of Her Majesty the Queen*, Windsor, 1995.

Millar 1963 Oliver Millar, *The Tudor, Stuart and Early Georgian Pictures in the Collection of Her Majesty the Queen*, London, 1969, 2 vols.

Miller 2003 James Miller, *Fertile Fortune: The Story of Tyntesfield*, London, 2003.

Murdoch 1981 John Murdoch, Jim Murrell, Patrick J. Noon & Roy Strong, *The English Miniature*, New Haven, 1981.

Murdoch 1997 John Murdoch, *Seventeenth-century English miniatures in the collection of the Victoria and Albert Museum*, London, 1997.

Ormond 1973 Richard Ormond, *Early Victorian Portraits*, London, 1973.

***Overbeck's* 2004** Hugh Meller, Vicki Pepper and Nick Stewart, *Overbeck's Museum and Garden*, NT guidebook, 2004.

Rees 1912 Rev. Thomas Mardy Rees, *Welsh Painters, Engravers, Sculptors (1527–1911)*, Carnarvon, 1912.

Reynolds 1971 Graham Reynolds, *Nicholas Hilliard and Isaac Oliver*, London, 1971.

Sadleir 1924 Thomas V. Sadleir, *An Irish Peer on the Continent (1801–1803); being a narrative of the tour of Stephen, 2nd Earl Mount Cashell, through France, Italy, etc., as related by Catherine Wilmot*, London, 1924.

St Aubyn 1978 John St Aubyn, *St Michael's Mount: illustrated history* *and guide*, St Michael's Mount, 1978.

Schäffers-Bodenhausen and Tiethoff-Spliethoff 1993 Karen Schäffers-Bodenhausen and Marieke Tiethoff-Spliethoff, *The Portrait Miniatures in the Collection of the House of Orange-Nassau*, Zwolle, 1993.

Schidlof 1964 Leo R. Schidlof, *The Miniature in Europe in the 16th, 17th, 18th, and 19th Centuries*, Graz, 1964.

Sharp 1996 Richard Sharp, *The Engraved Record of the Jacobite Movement*, Aldershot, 1996.

Spence 1997 Richard T. Spence, *Lady Anne Clifford*, Stroud, 1997.

***Stuarts* 1992** Anon., *La Cour des Stuarts à Saint-Germain-en-Laye au temps de Louis XIV*, exh. cat., Saint-Germain-en-Laye, 1992.

Stucley 1983 John Stucley, *Sir Bevil Grenville and his times 1596–1643*, Chichester, 1983.

Thieme-Becker 1907–50 Ulrich Thieme & Felix Becker, *Allgemeines Lexicon der bildenden künstler von der Antike bis zur Gegenwart*, Leipzig, 37 vols.

***Trerice* 2000** Michael Trinick, *Trerice*, NT guidebook, 2000.

***Tyntesfield* 2002** Francis Greenacre, *Tyntesfield*, NT guidebook, 2002.

***Van Dyck* 2004** Susan J. Barnes, Nora De Poorter, Oliver Millar & Horst Vey, *Van Dyck: A Complete Catalogue of the Paintings*, New Haven & London, 2004.

Walker 1992 Richard Walker, *The Eighteenth and Early Nineteenth Century Miniatures in the collection of Her Majesty the Queen*, London, 1992.

Williamson 1918 George Charles Williamson, *Life and Works of Ozias Humphry, R.A.*, London and New York, 1918.

Williamson and Engleheart 1902 George Charles Williamson and Henry Engleheart, *George Engleheart 1750–1829: Miniature Painter to George III*, London, 1902.

Wood 1789–1809 William Wood, *Memorandum of Miniatures*, MS, Victoria & Albert Museum library.

ABBREVIATIONS

attr.	attributed
BI	British Institution
bt.	bought
cat.	catalogue number
cf	compare
col.	colour
d.	daughter or died
DNB	*Dictionary of National Biography*
eng.	engraving
engr.	engraved
exh.	exhibited
HL	half length
HS	head and shoulders
inscr.	inscribed
Lit.	literature
m.	married
MSS	manuscripts
NG	National Gallery
NPG	National Portrait Gallery, London
opp.	opposite
pl.	plate
Prov	provenance
RA	Royal Academy, London
repr.	reproduced
RSA	Royal Society of Arts
s.	son
s/d	signed
SMP	Society of Miniature Painters
TQL	three quarter length
vol.	volume
WL	whole length
yst.	youngest

PICTURE CREDITS

Photographs of miniatures

© NTPL / Angelo Hornak
ALA 1-11; ARL 1-6 & 8-14; KIL 1-8; KNI 1-2;
LAN 1-5, 7-10 & 12-14; SMM 2-25; TRE 1

© Private Collection
ANT 1-17, 19-23, 25-29, 31, 33-44

© NTPL / David Garner
ANT 18, 24, 30 & 32; ARL 7; COS 1-12; OVE 1;
TYN 1-17, 20-22 & 24-28

© NTPL / Brenda Norrish
CDO 1-12, LAN 6 & 11

© NTPL / John Hammond
LYT 1-2; TYN 18-19 & 23

NTPL = National Trust Photographic Library

Photographs of houses

p.8 *(left)* NTPL / John Blake
(right) NTPL / Geoffrey Frosh

p.12 *(left)* NTPL / Derek Croucher
(right) NTPL / Andreas von Einsiedel

p.24 *(left)* NTPL / Matthew Antrobus
(right) NTPL / Andreas von Einsiedel

p.30 *(left)* NTPL / Chris Gascoigne
(right) NTPL / James Mortimer

p.34 *(left)* NTPL / Andrew Butler
(right) NTPL / Dennis Gilbert

p.42 *(left)* NTPL / Rupert Truman
(right) NTPL / Andreas von Einsiedel

p.44 *(left)* NTPL / Rupert Truman
(right) NTPL / Andreas von Einsiedel

p.49 *(left)* NTPL / Nick Meers
(right) NTPL / Nadia Mackenzie

p.51 *(left)* National Trust
(right) NTPL / Chris Vile

p.53 *(left)* NTPL / Oliver Benn
(right) NTPL / John Bethell

p.62 *(left)* NTPL / Andreas von Einsiedel
(right) NTPL / Oliver Benn

p.63 *(left)* NTPL / Andrew Butler
(right) NTPL / Andreas von Einsiedel

NTPL = National Trust Photographic Library

INDEX OF ARTISTS

Bold print indicates artists with definite or attributed work in the collection. Ordinary print means artists otherwise mentioned. Square brackets denote that a miniature is privately owned.

min. = miniaturist
pp. = portrait painter

BRITISH SCHOOL
seventeenth century: ALA **1**; [ANT **8**, **11**, **12**, **13**]; [SMM **2**]
eighteenth century: ALA **2-5**, **7** & **9**; ARL **1**; LAN **5**; [SMM **10-11**, **13**, **19**]; TYN **1**
nineteenth century: ALA **11**; [ANT **33**, **36-38**, **40**]; ARL **9-10**, **12**; COS **4-5** & **7**; KIL **3**, **8**; LAN **8**, **12-13**; LYT **1-2**; [SMM **7-8**, **25**]; TYN **6**, **16-17**, **21**
twentieth century: ARL **14**

BUCK, Adam (1759–1833), Irish min., born and worked in Cork, settled in London and exh. there 1795–1833, mainly miniatures and small portraits in pencil and watercolour. An extreme proponent of the Neo-classical style, he also issued the first instalment of an intended book on Greek vase-painting in 1812 LAN **10**

BUCK, Frederick (1771–*c.*1840), Irish min., younger brother of Adam Buck, worked in Cork, which was a major military centre and port of embarkation for troops in Napoleon's Wars, giving him a regular clientele of officers LYT 1

C., A. (fl.*c.*1900–05), possibly a miniaturist working from a photograph [ANT **44**]

CANALETTO, Giovanni Antonio Canal (1697–1768), Italian view painter TYN 13

CARWARDINE, Penelope (*c.*1730–1801), min., usually signing with initials *PC*, her women portraits often with long swan-like necks ALA 7; LAN 4

CHALMERS, Sir George, Bt. (1720–91), pp., Jacobite heraldic artist, with a doubtful title, who learnt portraiture and practised in Hull *c.*1777–81 ARL 1

CHALON, Alfred Edward (1780–1860), pp. and min.; exh. RA 1801–60; ARA 1812, RA 1816; appointed Portrait Painter to Queen Victoria 1837 KNI **1**

CHASE, Gordon (fl.1906), min., painting in gouache on ceramic CDO **1-10**

CHÉRON, Marie Anne (1649–before 1718), French min., a Huguenot convert to Catholicism, married when aged 52, Alexis-Simon Belle, portrait painter to the Old Pretender [ANT 15]

CHICHESTER, Rosalie (1865–1949), amateur artist; bequeathed Arlington Court, with its contents and surrounding estate, to the National Trust in 1949 ARL **11**

CHINNERY, George (1774–1852), Irish painter specialising in portraits and Chinese scenes, but infrequently as a min.; worked in Dublin, London and, from 1802, India [SMM **23**]

COLONE, Adam de (fl.1622–28), pp., son of Adriaen Vanson, 'His Majesty's painter' in Scotland 1580–1601, and Susanna de Colone. Trained in the Netherlands, but returned to Scotland around 1622 [SMM 2]

COMERFORD, John (*c.*1770–1832), born in Kilkenny, the most successful and prolific min. to spend his whole career in Ireland; exh. Dublin 1800–13 and London 1804 and 1809; much influenced by George Chinnery, who worked in Dublin 1795–1802, his miniatures sometimes have the appearance of small oil paintings, with loose brushwork and brown shading [SMM 23]

CONTINENTAL SCHOOL
nineteenth century: LAN **9**

COOPER, Alexander (*c.*1609–*c.*1660), elder brother of the more famous Samuel Cooper, their mother being a sister of John Hoskins ALA 1

COOPER, Samuel (1609–72), min., nephew and pupil of John Hoskins; he became the foremost miniaturist of the seventeenth century, working at the courts of both Charles I and Charles II; his miniature of Oliver Cromwell is generally recognised as one of the great portraits of the world (*see* Murdoch 1981, pp.104-20) [ANT 7, **9**, **10**]

COSWAY, Richard (1742–1821), min., born in Devon, exh. RA 1770–1806, appointed ARA 1770 and RA 1771. His portrait of Mrs Fitzherbert immediately attracted the attention of the Prince of Wales, who appointed him as his official miniature painter in 1786 and general adviser for the decoration of Carlton House. From then, his future as a fashionable miniature painter was assured, but he lost the

Prince's favour in 1811, his eyesight began to fail, and he spent his last years amassing material for an autobiography and an account of miniature painting, of which neither was published. Cosway's wife Maria is believed to have copied some of his work, which was much admired and copied by other artists, such as the Plimers, George Engleheart, William Wood, Anne Mee and Charlotte Jones (*see* Stephen Lloyd, *Richard & Maria Cosway*, exh.cat., Scottish National Portrait Gallery, Edinburgh, 1995). A genuine Cosway miniature is recognisable from its quality, the three-dimensional illusion achieved by modelling with long curved brushstrokes, the transparent colouring, and the vivid azure sky background ARL 3; TYN 5

COTES, Samuel (1734–1818), min., younger brother of the portrait painter, Francis Cotes; exh. in London 1760–89, including the first RA exh. 1769. His initials *S.C.*, with which he usually signed his miniatures, have led to confusion with the Irish miniaturist, Samuel Collins TYN 1

CROSS, Peter (*c.*1645–1716), min., the subject of some confusion due to his habit of signing with the monogram *PC*, which looks very like the monogram *LC*, formerly associated with a mythical artist, Lawrence Cross [ANT 8]

CROSSE, Richard (1742–1810), pp. and min., born in Devon, exh. in London 1760–96, mainly portraits in oil and miniatures in watercolour. He was appointed Enamel Painter to George III in *c.*1788. A greenish-blue colour in the shading is one of his recognisable characteristics. His ledger was transcribed by Long in the *Walpole Society Journal*, vol.XVII (1929), pp.61-94 LAN 8; [SMM **14**, 15, **16**]

D'AGAR, Charles (1669–1723), French pp., son of the painter Jacques d'Agar (1642–1715), born in Paris, worked in England as a young man with his father, 1681–*c.*1684, followed him to Copenhagen, but returned to England in 1691 and died in London [ANT 14]

DAHL, Michael (*c.*1659–1743), Swedish pp., worked mainly in London, where he probably influenced his fellow countrymen Charles Boit and Christian Richter to take up enamel painting [ANT 16, 20]; LAN 1

DALTON, Magdalena (*see* ROSS)

DIXON, Annie (1817–1901), min., born at Horncastle; exh. RA 1844–93, mainly miniature portraits, including several of the Royal Family [ANT **34**]

DIXON, Nicholas (*c.*1645–after 1708), min., succeeded Samuel Cooper as Keeper of the King's Picture Closet and Limner to Charles II (*see* Reynolds 1988, pp.81-6) [ANT 8]; [SMM **5**]

DOBSON, William (1611–46), pp., introduced to Charles I by Van Dyck, appointed Sergeant Painter 1641, accompanied the King to Oxford, where he painted Royalists [SMM 4]

DUPRÉ (fl.*c.*1820–40), French min. LAN **11**

DUPRÉ, Louis (1789–1837), French painter LAN 11

EDRIDGE, Henry (1769–1821), pp. and min., exh. RA 1786–1821, especially small drawings in pencil and watercolour [SMM 18, 22]

EGLEY, William (1798–1870), min., largely self-taught; exh. in London 1824–69, usually signing on the back of his miniatures with his address [ANT **35**]

EINSLIE, Samuel (fl.1785–1808), min., exh. RA 1785–1808; painted portraits and miniatures, and executed mezzotints, some of which were copied from the works of Gainsborough and Hoppner KIL **2**

ELLISSEN, Irene (*see* BEGBIE)

ENGLEHEART, George (1750–1829), studied under Sir Joshua Reynolds, exh. RA 1773–1822; his fee books (still in the family collection) and the RA catalogues record nearly 5,000 miniatures painted in forty-nine years COS 2

ENGLISH SCHOOL
seventeenth century: [SMM **4**]

ERSKINE, Lady Mary Henrietta (d.1820), min., daughter of Sir Henry Erskine, 5th Bt. and sister of James, 2nd Earl of Rosslyn; died unmarried KIL **5-6**, 7-8

FERGUSON, James (1710–76), born in Banffshire of poor parents and had little education; studied the stars when looking after sheep, whence his later subriquet of 'Ferguson the astronomer'. Learnt to draw in Edinburgh, then came south; min. but worked mainly in 'China ink' (i.e. Indian ink), drawing portraits (in 1746) for 9 shillings at home, or half-a-guinea at the sitter's (by 1752, 12s 6d and 15s) ALA **6**

FRENCH SCHOOL
eighteenth century: LAN **2-3**
nineteenth century: [ANT **28**, **31**]; ARL **12**

GERMAN SCHOOL
nineteenth century: COS **6**
twentieth century: ARL **13**

GIBSON, Mary Josephine (fl.1906), min. CDO **11-12**

GIBSON, Richard (1615–90), min., dwarf page to Charles I and Henrietta Maria; painted by Van Dyck; painted several portraits of Oliver Cromwell [ANT 7]

GOYEN, Jan Josefsz Van (1596–1656), Dutch landscape painter and pp. KNI 2

GRAVES, Hon. Henry Richard (1818–82), pp., third son of the courtier, Thomas, 2nd Baron Graves, and Lady Mary Paget; worked in London, exh. RA 1846–81 [ANT 38]

HARDIE, Charles (1858–1916), Scottish pp., studied at RSA Life School in Edinburgh, exh. RA 1885–1903 CDO 2

HARDING, H.J. (fl.1823–25), min., exh. RA and Suffolk Street 1823–25 TYN **15**

HENREY, Lucas Edwin (fl.1898), min. KNI **2**

HILLIARD, Laurence (1581/2–1647/8), min., son of Nicholas Hilliard [ANT **2**, **4**]

HILLIARD, Nicholas (1547–1619), famous Elizabethan min., and author of *The Arte of Limning* [ANT **1**, 2, 4]

HOGARTH, William (1697–1764), England's most ambitious and original painter and engraver in the 18th century TYN 2

HOLLAR, Wenceslaus (1607–77), draughtsman and engraver, born in Prague, came to England in 1636 [SMM 3]

HONE, Nathaniel (1718–84), min. and pp., born in Dublin, son of a merchant and descendant of Dutch goldsmiths, succeeded C.F. Zincke as the leading enamel miniaturist of the day; exh. in London 1760–84, a founder member of the RA, he gave up painting miniatures in about 1770 to concentrate on full-scale portraits in oil [SMM 18]; TYN 4

HOSKINS, John (*c*.1595–1664/5), min., known to have been painting miniature portraits in *c*.1615; appointed 'His Majesty's Limner' in 1640 [ANT 5]; [SMM **3**]

HOSKINS, John the Younger (1615/20–after 1690), min., of whom little is known, apart from a group of signed miniatures in the Buccleuch Collection, and signed examples of his work at Ickworth (NT) and Madresfield [ANT **6**]

HOWARD, Annie (d.1915), min., exh. in London 1859–1903 [ANT **39**, **41**]

HUGHES, George (fl.1813–58), painted portraits, landscapes and miniatures in London TYN **20**

HUMPHRY, Ozias (1742–1810), pp. and min., born in Devon, exh. in Bath and London 1762–97, worked in India 1785–88; painted in oil, crayon and watercolour, his best work being before 1771, when his eyes were damaged by a fall from his horse; painted nothing after 1797, when his eyesight failed totally ALA **10**; [ANT 23]; [SMM **12**]; TYN **3**

ITALIAN SCHOOL
nineteenth century: ARL **8**; LAN **14**

JACKSON, John (1778–1831), British pp., exh. RA 1804–30; ARA 1815, RA 1817 LAN 10

JAGGER, Charles (*c*.1770–1827), min., worked mainly in Bath; his

the RA and exh. there 1769–83, miniatures, enamels and watercolour drawings. Enamel and Miniature Painter to George III and Queen Charlotte. His style is easily recognisable from its linear shading, angularity of drawing, protruding lips and small eyes [SMM **15**]

MIEREVELDT, Michel Van (1567–1641), Dutch pp. (after) [ANT 3]

MILES, Edward (1752–1828), min., Miniature Painter to Queen Charlotte and Tsar Alexander I TRE **1**

NEWTON, Sir William (1785–1869), min., born in London, exh. RA and BI 1808–63; appointed Miniature Painter to William IV and Queen Adelaide in 1833, and knighted by Queen Victoria in 1837 [ANT **24**, **32**]; ARL **5**

NIXON, James (*c.*1741–1812), Scottish min., lived in Devonshire; Miniature Painter to Prince Regent [SMM **17**]

NOBLE, Matthew (1818–76), sculptor, born in Yorkshire, studied in London as a pupil of John Francis, made his name with his Wellington Monument in Manchester (1856); exh. RA 1845–76 [ANT 36]

NORTHCOTE, James (1746–1831), pp., worked in studio of Reynolds, whose conversation he recorded; travelled in Italy 1777–80; RA 1787 TYN 1-2, 4

OLIVER, Isaac (*c.*1565–1617), min., son of a Huguenot goldsmith who moved to London in 1568; pupil of Nicholas Hilliard; worked for Queen Anne of Denmark and her son, Henry, Prince of Wales, establishing a thriving court practice [ANT 2]

OLIVER, Peter (1598–1647), min., eldest son of Isaac Oliver, and copyist in miniature of pictures in Charles I's collection [SMM **1**]

OPIE, John (1761–1807), Cornish pp. and historical painter, the protégé of William Wolcot ('Peter Pindar'); moved to London 1780, where Wolcot made him fashionable as 'the Cornish wonder'; exh. RA from 1782, ARA 1786, RA 1787 [SMM 18, 21-22]

OWEN, J. (fl. early 19th century), landscape painter TYN **10-13**

OWEN, Jacob (1778–1870), architect TYN 10

OWEN, William (1769–1825), the best and most serious pp. after Lawrence, he became Portrait Painter to the Prince of Wales on the death of Hoppner in 1810; crippled after 1820 KIL 3

PAYE, Elizabeth (Mrs Bryane) (fl.1798–1811), min. [ANT **25-26**]; LAN **7**

PENNY, Edward (1714–91), pp. and history painter (esp. of uplifiting subjects), exh. RA 1762–82 [ANT 17, 19]

PETITOT, Jean (1607–91), min., one of the greatest enamelists of the seventeenth century, patronised by Louis XIV and the French Court for over forty years COS 1

PHILLIP, John (1817–67), Scottish pp., known as 'Spanish Phillip', from his paintings of Iberian subjects ARA 1857, RA 1859 TYN 17

PICKERSGILL, Henry William (1782–1875), pp., member of a dynasty of painters, exh. RA & BI 1806– 72; ARA 1822, RA 1826 KNI 1

PLIMER, Andrew (1763–1837), min., born in Shropshire, went to London in 1781 and employed as a manservant to Richard Cosway; exh. RA 1786–1830. He made frequent tours to the West Country and Scotland. Painted usually on large ivories, the faces with long noses, wide-open eyes, dark complexions, and thin cross-hatching in the background ARL **3**; LAN **6**

P., M. (fl. *c.*1917), a min. signing with the initials *M.P.* (or *M.R.*) may have worked in a photographic studio TYN **28**

POUSSIN, Nicolas (1594–1665), classic French history and landscape painter KNI 2

PREWETT, William (fl.1733–60), min., probably a pupil of Zincke [ANT **17-19**]; [SMM 8]

RAMSAY, Allan (1713–84), Scottish pp., trained in Italy, worked in Edinburgh and London, appointed Portrait Painter to George III 1767 [SMM 12]

THOURON, Jacques (1740–89), Swiss min., worked in Paris; exh Salon 1781–82 [SMM 18]

TOUTIN, Henri (1746–1832), Dutch min. [ANT 3]

TOMASICH Y HARO, Antonio (1820–90), Spanish min., worked in Madrid, Mexico, Havana and London. He probably met William Gibbs in Spain, where Gibbs managed the family business for many years in Cadiz. A miniature of William Gibbs, signed and dated 1872, was sold at Sotheby's, 12 December 1966 TYN 17, **24-27**

VANDERBANK, John (*c.*1694–1739), highly distinctive British pp., history painter and illustrator (after) [SMM 8]

VAN DYCK, Sir Anthony (1599–1641), pupil and onetime assistant of Rubens, history painter and pp., who founded the tradition of English portraiture [ANT 1, 4]; after KIL 2; [SMM 3]

VERTUE, George (1684–1756), engraver and antiquary, official engraver to the Society of Antiquaries 1717–56, and the first English art historian TYN 2

VINCI, Leonardo da (1452–1519), Italian painter, sculptor, architect and *uomo universale* LAN 7

WEBLING, Ethel (fl.1880–1903), min., worked in London [ANT **43**]

WEBSTER, Joseph Samuel (d.1796), pp., probable pupil of Thomas Hudson, whose manner he adopted, worked in London [ANT 22]

WINTERHALTER, Franz Xaver (1805–73), German pp., exh. RA 1852–67; painted royal families of France, England, Belgium, Germany, Austria and Russia [ANT 36]

WOLLASTON, Hannah (fl.*c.*1760), min., possibly the daughter of the portrait-painter John Wollaston Sr. TYN **2**

WOLLASTON, John, Jr. (fl.1742–75), pp., emigrated to North America *c.*1749, but returned to England 1767 TYN 2

WOLLASTON, John, Sr. (*c.*1672–after 1742), pp. and musician TYN 2

WYKES, H. (fl.*c.*1880–90), min. OVE **1**

ZEICH (fl.1780–5?), Polish min. [ANT **21**]

ZINCKE, Christian Frederick (1683/4–1767), min., apprenticed to his father, a goldsmith of Dresden; settled in London to work at enamel painting, and probably taught by Charles Boit, to whose practice he succeeded when Boit left for France in 1714; appointed Enamel Painter to Frederick, Prince of Wales in 1727 [ANT 17]

INDEX OF SITTERS